6th August

John,

Perhaps this
will help.

Rich

THE TEACH YOURSELF BOOKS
EDITED BY LEONARD CUTTS

GOLF

TEACH YOURSELF
GOLF

By
J. C. JESSOP
M.A., Ph.D.

THE ENGLISH UNIVERSITIES PRESS LTD
102 NEWGATE STREET
LONDON · E C 1

First Printed . . 1950
Second Edition . . 1960
This impression (revised) 1964

Printed and bound in Great Britain for the English Universities
Press Ltd., by Butler & Tanner Ltd., Frome and London

CONTENTS

ACKNOWLEDGMENT

THE author and the publishers are greatly indebted to the Rules of Golf Committee of the Royal and Ancient Golf Club of St. Andrews for permission to print the rules of the game as an appendix to this book. These rules are copyright by the Royal and Ancient Golf Club and must not be reproduced in any form without their permission.

CHAPTER I

INTRODUCTORY

A COMMON complaint lodged against text books and articles on how to play golf is that they are too complicated and too technical. Even many intelligent readers confess that they find themselves struggling with, and wallowing in, a welter of ideas that to them seem confusing, confounding, and even conflicting.

It must be clearly understood that this book is designed primarily for beginners, that is, for those who have never played and for those whose knowledge of the game is but little. At the same time, the writer has kept in mind the ordinary player who, it is hoped, may find some advice or suggestions that may be useful. The writer is well aware that books, at best, are poor substitutes for good teachers. We can learn from books, but the teacher with his pupil before him has a better understanding of his pupil, and can employ methods and practices that are denied to a writer. The teacher can adapt and adjust his presentation according to the needs of the pupil. Furthermore, diagrams and illustrations can

7

enlighten, but they cannot replace reality ; they portray only certain aspects of reality to the exclusion of all others. Nevertheless, no matter how good the teacher or the instruction, the fact remains that the learner must do his own learning. That is incontrovertible. To develop his inborn capacity and to realize his innate potentialities he must apply not only diligence but what is more important, his intelligence.

That you can teach yourself golf cannot be denied. With very few exceptions, the best golfers all the world over taught themselves. They began as youngsters, many of them acting as caddies during their school holidays and at week-ends. Interested in the game, as most caddies are, it was natural for them not only to swing a club but to swing it after the manner of the best players they served or saw. Briefly, they learned by imitation. Practice, experience, knowledge of the game, chiefly derived from their own experience, and a natural aptitude, all fitted to lay the foundation of their success. But these factors in themselves are not enough : temperament, mental attitude, diligence, courage, and self-discipline all combine to form an important part in the make-up of a successful golfer.

Imitation, it will be granted, plays a large part in learning. All of us have an inherent tendency to imitate ; we do so wittingly or unwittingly. If we are to imitate we must find suitable models or appropriate patterns. It would be incongruous for an elderly, stout person to try to imitate or emulate all the actions of any of the present-day champions. Age and physical attributes have to be taken into consideration. For example, what is possible or easy for a tall, slim person may be well-nigh impossible for another who is short and stout. The models in these extreme cases will naturally vary. Yet there are fundamental principles which the young and the not so young, the tall and the short, the stout and the slim, will have to follow if they are to meet with any degree of success. The aim and purpose of this primer is to try to give some guidance and provide some helpful suggestions. No attempt has been made to dogmatize. The writer fully appreciates the maxim, " When two do the same thing, it is not the same thing after all."

We learn by doing. " Practice makes perfect." Not necessarily, but perfection cannot be attained without practice. The most effective way of learning is to experiment. By so doing, the learner will not only understand, but, and this is important, he will retain more readily what he has learned. Practice and theory should rarely be divorced. Too much theory can defeat its own end ; there cannot be too much practice, provided it is diligent and intelligent. Mental activity should accompany motor activity. Many can learn only by practice because they lack the mental capacity to understand oral or verbal explanations, or become confused when faced with a problem. We can try, try, and try again, learning all the time not only by our success but also by our failure. It is a good method but slow—slow compared with that of accepting the advice and following the example of those who are proficient. This is second-hand as distinct from first-hand experience. A learner should never depend entirely upon second-hand experience, that is, the experience of others. We can derive greater benefit by making use of both. Just as we have an inborn tendency to imitate, so we have an innate propensity to accept ideas suggested by others. Exposition, demonstration, and suggestion on the part of the teacher, and imitation on the part of the learner, combined with the desire to find out for himself, can all arouse the learner's mental activity. Without this no one can learn.

Do not imagine that you will make rapid and regular progress. There will come times when you will think that you are making no progress. You may feel that you have lost any skill you had acquired. The success you expected seems to have vanished, and you will naturally be disappointed. You may lose interest and even give up—a fatal mistake. All learners go through this experience in the acquisition not only of skill but of knowledge. This is the time that the teacher, by his advice and encouragement, can be helpful. The pupil will be made to realize that more drill-work is necessary. He must practise intelligently, and if he does so he will find that drill-work or practice is neither dull nor monotonous. Practice in time becomes second nature.

Practice has its different uses. We may practise to try to reach perfection; we may practise to eradicate faults. Eminent pianists practise for hours daily to keep themselves up to concert pitch. How many eminent British golfers practise when they are playing well or, as they say, on the top of their game? Very few. It is a mistaken notion that one should practise only to correct faults. It is essential to practise, and to keep on practising, that which we can do well so that we can at least maintain that standard. It is then that we can note just exactly how we achieve the best results; and having learned to accomplish this through our own efforts, practical and theoretical, we shall more readily retain and remember just what we must do to bring about the results desired. Diligent and intelligent practice is everything; it is the best of all instructors; and without it there can be no perfection.

CHAPTER II

A SET OF CLUBS:
COMPLETE AND SKELETON

A NON-GOLFER is bound to be amazed when, for the first time, he sees the set or kit of any leading amateur or professional. He will be surprised at the number and variety of the clubs, and he will no doubt be impressed by the size of the bag and its bulging attachments. And if he tries to lift it he will be staggered.

Some years ago the number of clubs to be used in competitions was limited to fourteen. Prior to this, some Americans were carrying as many as twenty, and some even more. The United States Golf Association also restricts the number of clubs to fourteen, but in tournaments not sponsored by the U.S.G.A. most professionals use sixteen. In the Masters' Tournament only fourteen clubs are allowed. As might be expected, there was considerable argument and discussion before the maximum was fixed at fourteen. Many would like this number reduced ; and the older players particularly would reduce it by half. It is interesting to note that in 1948 the English Golf Union recommended the County Unions to encourage their Clubs to hold com-

petitions in which the number of clubs each
player should carry should be limited to seven.
Golf Clubs and Golf Associations are perturbed
that the high cost of golf is debarring many,
particularly young people, from taking up the
game. It has since been reported in the Press that
English Golf Clubs and Associations are approximately fifty per cent in favour and fifty per cent
against the suggested seven-club scheme. The
English Golf Union has reported that the Artisan
Golfers' Association and the National Association of Public Golf Courses are in favour, but that
a fair number of replies favoured a limit of eight
or nine clubs. Competitions held with a limit of
seven clubs all indicated that the scoring was quite
as low as it would have been with a full set.

The set of the majority of golfers comprises
fewer than the limit allowed. Most golfers carry
their own clubs, especially these days when golf
requisites are much more expensive, and caddies'
fees are much higher than they used to be.* The
sensible golfer limits himself to a kit which he
can comfortably carry. Yet how often do we see
a " duffer ", with more money than sense, hacking
his way round a course with a complete outfit ?

Let us consider, first, a set of clubs consisting
of the maximum number, fourteen. There are
two main types, generally known as the " woods "

* Hence the popularity of the modern convenience, the
caddie-car.

and the "irons". The woods comprise the driver, brassie, and spoon, or, as they are sometimes called, woods Nos. 1, 2, and 3 respectively. There is another wood called the No. 4; it is really another spoon, only slightly shorter and with a little more loft than the ordinary spoon or No. 3 wood. The irons, all graduated in loft, are numbered 1, 2, 3, 4, 5, 6, 7, 8, excluding the putter, and a special club variously described as a sand-wedge or blaster. These fourteen clubs make up a complete set. Some players make a slightly different selection according to preference. Few players now carry a No. 1 iron; some do not include a No. 4 wood. Fred Daly's irons range from No. 2 to No. 10; he thereby increases the number of clubs for short-range shots. In tournaments not sponsored by the U.S.G.A. Ben Hogan uses sixteen clubs: four woods, irons 1 to 9, a pitch-wedge, a sand-wedge, and a putter. The nature of the course determines largely which two clubs are to be excluded when the limit is fourteen; the pitch-wedge is likely to be one of them, and, incidentally, Hogan prefers his spoon (No. 3) to his brassie.

Let us now consider what a minimum or skeleton set should comprise. Taking the woods first, a beginner would require one at least, preferably a spoon (No. 3). And as for irons, a No. 3, No. 5, No. 7, and a putter would be sufficient. Our skeleton set would then consist of five clubs. Our open champions in the first two decades of the present century carried only seven or eight clubs. Do not buy any odd clubs or a mixed set. It is better to purchase a few that are " matched ", and as you progress you can add to your set from time to time, choosing the club of which you stand in most need.

If you join a Golf Club you should buy your clubs from the professional attached to the Club. He depends on the Club members for his livelihood and should be supported. If your clubs at any time require repairs he will naturally be more pleased to do them knowing you have purchased your clubs from him. He will, incidentally, take more interest in your clubs and your game, and it will pay you directly and indirectly to support him. The professional will advise you as to the type of club that will suit you best. He will consider your age, height and physique ; he will judge whether you should have clubs that are upright or flat in lie ; he will also consider the weight and balance. He will choose shafts that have some spring or whip ; the older you are the whippier shaft you will need. The spring in the shaft helps those particularly who have not the strength or suppleness in the wrists to whip the head of the club through with sufficient speed. It is speed rather than strength that determines the distance the ball will be driven, provided, of course, it is hit accurately.

Many players do not take due care of their clubs. You can buy covers to protect the heads of your wooden clubs, and it is worth while to do so. The covers protect them from being marked or damaged through being knocked against each other, and they help to keep them dry. If you carry your own clubs, don't throw the bag down before you play a stroke ; it is just as easy, if not easier, to place it, and there will be less chance of marking your clubs. Don't use your clubs as a rest and lean on them ; you are putting unnecessary strain on the shafts. If your clubs have become wet you should dry them before putting them back in your locker.

When the heads of your wooden clubs begin to lose their high polish you can restore it by using a little furniture cream. This will make the heads look like new, and will act as a preservative. If the grips of your clubs are leather and become dry and hard, a little castor oil will moisten and soften them, but see that you give it time to be absorbed before you play your next game. You will find that the grips will feel more kindly to the hands. The latest grips are made of all-weather material and, of course, you should not use castor oil on these.

The good tennis player looks after his racquet ; the good batsman cares for his bat ; and the good golfer does not neglect his clubs.

CHAPTER III

THE GRIP

THE grip you adopt should be determined largely by the nature of your hands. As the size of the hands and the length and strength of the fingers vary from person to person, it is natural that the same grip will not suit everyone. Because Harry Vardon used a particular grip with great success it became fashionable to adopt his grip. It must be remembered, however, that Vardon had extraordinarily large hands. The important thing about the grip is that the hands should be placed properly in relation to each other. As the two hands must work in unison they should be held close together, but it is the fingers mainly that hold and control the club. The club lies across the base of the last three fingers of the right hand and almost diagonally across the palm of the left hand. The forefinger of the right hand is crooked round the shaft so that it lies on the second joint. The position of the forefinger is similar to that on a trigger. The club also lies across the second joint of the left forefinger. The thumbs of each hand should be placed slightly

across, not down, the shaft, with the left thumb
bedded in the palm of the right hand.   In the

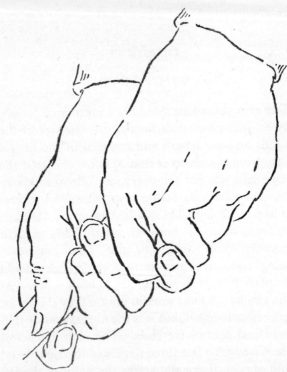

Overlapping grip, side view, little finger of right hand overlapping forefinger of left hand.   Right forefinger crooked
round shaft, triggerwise ; left thumb is bedded in palm of
right hand.

Vardon grip the little finger of the right hand
overlaps the forefinger of the left hand.   The
last three fingers of the left hand and the thumb

and forefinger of the right hand exert most pressure in gripping the club.

The hands are not only close but opposed to each other. You will have a good idea whether your hands are correctly placed if the Vs formed by the thumbs and forefingers of each hand are in line with the shaft. This was the position of the hands of Vardon and of Jones. Cotton's position is similar but most of the leading Americans have the Vs pointing a little more to the right, more towards the right shoulder. The reason for this slight difference is discussed later in our chapter on Hooking. The Vardon grip is now generally called the " overlapping " grip to distinguish it from the " interlocking " grip.

Some eminent golfers find that the interlocking grip suits them better. In the interlocking grip the little finger of the right hand and the forefinger of the left hand are interlocked. The left thumb may lie across the shaft bedded in the palm of the right hand, as in the Vardon grip, or it may be placed round the shaft resting on the second finger of the same hand.

Either of these grips, the overlapping or the interlocking, gives a feeling of compactness. Sandy Herd and that mighty hitter, Abe Mitchell, neither overlapped nor interlocked. Mitchell appeared to overlap, as the forefinger of his left hand was not round the shaft but crooked so that the point of the forefinger rested underneath the shaft, the shaft lying across the point of the finger. It has been advocated by no less an authority than Bobby Jones that those whose hands are small or weak, or whose fingers are not strong, may find that the old-fashioned grip suits them better. But no one could say that Herd or Mitchell had weak fingers or hands. The maxim followed by the old school was, " Tight with the left hand and slack with the right." When the right hand caught up with the left at impact the right hand automatically tightened its grip on the club. It is interesting to note that the famous American player, Byron Nelson, grips the club very firmly in both hands, with the left hand grasping the tighter. He maintains that this firmness is one of the real secrets of hitting a golf ball well. His thumb and forefinger of the right hand exert the pressure along with the last three fingers of the left hand.

A word of warning may be timely here. Beginners are inclined to hold the club too tightly with both hands. This is fatal. The muscles of the forearms and wrists become too tense. To produce the necessary speed in the swing, particularly just before and after impact, flexibility is essential. On the other hand, if the club is held too slackly, there will be a loss of control as the club is likely to turn in the hands. In the back swing the club should be held quite firmly, but not tightly, with the left hand, for it is the left hand that guides, steadies, and controls the club. And this is important : the club must be held firmly in the left hand at the top of the swing. There must be no loosening of the grip. On the other hand, the grip of the right hand with thumb and forefinger should be comparatively light at the top of the swing, at least with the wooden clubs, when length is desired. The club is held firmly in the left hand for all shots either with woods or with irons, but the thumb and forefinger of the right hand also grip the club firmly in playing most iron shots, but that will be considered later when dealing with these strokes.

Generally speaking, the woods should be held about half an inch from the end. This is the point where the balance of the club usually seems best and where, consequently, more control can be exercised. With the irons it is different because with them full shots are not always played. With the shorter irons particularly, a shorter grip is often necessary for better control.

If you are about to begin to play golf you should try, first, the Vardon or overlapping grip. It may seem a little awkward to begin with but it should soon feel comfortable and natural. It is compact and allows the hands to work in unison. If you have strong fingers you may prefer the interlocking grip. Instead of bedding the left thumb in the palm of the right hand you may find it more comfortable to place it round the shaft, especially if your thumb is straight and not very flexible.

It was by trial and error that Ben Hogan discovered the grip that suited him best. It differs from the Vardon grip in that the little finger of the right hand grips round the knuckle of the index finger of the left hand instead of overlapping it. His right hand in relation to the left is well on top; and the pressure of the right hand on the grip is with the two middle fingers, not with the thumb and forefinger. Like all good golfers he grips firmly with the last three fingers of the left hand.

Experiment and decide which type of grip you find most successful. The choice will largely be determined by the nature of your hands. Persevere preferably with the Vardon or overlapping grip before you try a change.

The Stance.

1. Open. 2. Closed. 3. Square.

The stance or position of the feet varies slightly according to the type of shot desired. The position of the ball in relation to the feet also varies. And, furthermore, the stance of the best players differs slightly according to individual preference.

Sometimes the right foot is a little in advance

1. SQUARE

HEELS IN LINE

2. OPEN

LEFT FOOT SLIGHTLY BACK

3. CLOSED

RIGHT FOOT SLIGHTLY BACK

of the left. This is called an "open" stance. When the left foot is in advance of the right, the stance is said to be "closed". Again, the stance may be " square ", that is, neither foot is in advance of the other.

The terms " open " and " closed " are misleading, apart from the fact they are antonyms or " opposites ". " Open " and " closed " might suggest that the feet are respectively wide apart and close together. The term " square " is a happier choice and can be more readily understood. As these terms are frequently used they should be clearly understood by the beginner.

The stance and the position of the ball in relation to the feet are dealt with in the various strokes described in this book. Generally speaking, for the wood shots the breadth of the shoulders should be the width of the stance. As the stroke decreases in length, so the feet are placed closer to each other. The same principle applies to the position of the feet and the ball : the shorter the stroke, the closer the feet to the ball. As the clubs used for the shorter shots are comparatively short, one must stand closer to the ball.

In the days when Vardon was supreme, most players, like him, used an open stance. An exception was his great contemporary, James Braid. Braid favoured a slightly closed stance. Bobby Jones used a square stance ; so does Henry Cotton. Byron Nelson, like most of his American contemporaries, favours a closed stance. Of these stances, the square is the safest. The open stance tends to slicing, that is, the ball in its flight swerves to the right. The closed stance may lead to " hooking ", that is, the ball in its flight swerves to the left. The closed stance is often adopted to get extra distance, as a ball that veers slightly to the left travels further than a straight ball, and much further than one that veers to the right. Expert players can exploit with advantage the different types of stance according to the particular kind of stroke they wish to play. Particular shots may demand either an open or closed stance, but for an ordinary straightforward shot a square stance is safest. The foregoing remarks apply particularly to driving or to long iron shots. The stance for approach shots will be dealt with under that particular heading. Even in normal circumstances the stance may vary according to preference. Byron Nelson, for instance, uses a slightly closed stance when playing his woods ; a square stance with long irons (Nos. 1, 2, 3) ; a slightly open stance with the medium irons (Nos. 4, 5, 6) ; and an open stance with the short irons (Nos. 7, 8, 9). Ben Hogan uses a slightly closed stance not only for his woods but for his long irons, including the No. 4. He considers the No. 5 iron is the iron dividing the long and the short irons ; and for the short irons he uses a slightly open stance.

We have said in the opening paragraph that

the position of the ball in relation to the feet also varies. Generally speaking, one may say that most golfers play the ball at a point opposite the left heel, but, as Jones says, " it is impossible to contend that the same relative positions of ball and feet are proper for everybody ". He found that the ball played from a point opposite the instep of his left foot suited him best. Hogan plays the ball further back, about two inches inside of the left heel. It is worth while to experiment with the ball a little further forward or backwards to see which position in relation to the feet gives you the best results. You will probably find that if you place the ball too far back your shot will be pushed out to the right, as the right hand has not had time to close the face of the club. On the other hand, if the ball is played from a position too far forward, the shot may fly to the left of the intended line of flight, as the right wrist may by then have begun to roll over the left. A slight adjustment in the position of the ball at the address may make a considerable difference.

As the beginner has so much to learn, it would probably be simpler for him to play all his shots, for some time at least, with the ball opposite the left heel. Later, he could experiment to find whether any slight adjustment to the left or right produces better results.

CHAPTER IV

THE WOODS

I. The Driver : the Swing

PROBABLY nothing pleases a beginner more than to hit a good drive. This is only natural, but he must realize that driving is not the be-all and end-all. The main and only concern of some players is to drive the ball a tremendous distance. They often do, but the ball frequently finishes deep in the rough or lost in the heather or gorse. The beginner should realize that golf tournaments are generally won on and near the green, and that it is accuracy rather than length that brings success. There is no advantage to be gained from a long drive if it finishes in the rough. A controlled tee-shot simplifies the second shot which, in turn, should make the next shot comparatively easy. The beginner cannot expect to control his shots. He must learn, first, to hit the ball, and hit it hard. Later on, with some adjustment of grip, stance, or swing, he should be able to command greater control.

On the other hand, if accuracy is the first essential, it would be better for the beginner to

start not with the driver but with one of the
medium irons. If he does so, he should choose
the No. 5 iron, and work up to the No. 3 iron,
the spoon, and then the driver. Few beginners,
however, will adopt this procedure because they
have what we believe to be a wrong conception
of the relative importance of driving. Iron play
and putting are at least equally important, but
it must be admitted that these will be of little
avail if the wood play is not accurate. Hogan
goes so far as to assert that " if there is one
department that is more important than the
others, it would probably be the wood shots ".
But it is not the wood shots that separate the
leading players. If so, there would be no
American supremacy, as all the leading players
drive consistently well. The Americans play the
short irons better and putt more consistently than
the leading British players. Therein lies the
difference.

We shall begin with the driver mainly because
that is the club with which the beginner usually
wishes to start. He would get quicker and better
results if he began with the spoon (No. 3 wood),
which is easier to play than the driver. The
reader, we hope, will by now have some idea of
the stance and the grip. We may recapitulate
briefly. There are three types of stance : the
closed, the open, and the square. The square
stance is recommended, but the beginner will

find from experiment which of these gives him the most satisfactory results. The overlapping grip is also recommended.

In addressing the ball, the player must relax. That is the first essential, and it cannot be over-emphasized. The beginner tends, first, to grip the club too tightly, and, secondly, to stand too stiffly. The muscles of the arms and legs are consequently too tense and taut. As the swing should be full, free, and rhythmical, this cannot be if the muscles are tense.

Having satisfied yourself that your grip is comfortable and that your muscles are relaxed, place the face of the driver immediately behind the ball, taking care that the face is square to the ball. The feet should be about shoulder width apart. If they are too far apart, hip action will be restricted ; if they are too close, balance may be upset. The ball at the address should be at a point opposite the left heel. The arms should not be fully extended but should hang fairly loosely. The hands should be slightly behind the ball. Hold the driver about half an inch from the end, as, generally, the balance is better there than when the club is held at the end. Then comes the little waggle at the address. The waggle or waggles help to loosen the muscles and give the player time to make any little adjustment in his stance, if necessary.

After the preliminary waggles, and just before

Feet shoulder width apart. " Toes " pointing slightly outwards.
Ball opposite left heel. Body erect, with knees slightly
bent. The Vs formed by thumbs and forefingers pointing
towards right shoulder.

the back swing is started, it is advisable to hold the face of the driver square to the ball for a second. This momentary pause helps the player to concentrate on the ball, as it is very important to keep the eye on it during the back swing and the down swing until impact.

The start of the back swing is all-important, for without a good start there can be no full and rhythmic swing. How is it begun ? This is a very difficult question, and it cannot be answered categorically. To the ordinary spectator the leading players appear to start the back swing in the same way, but a close study of their swings reveals slight differences. Cotton admits that he does not always adopt the same method. For a time he may start first with the hands dragging the club-head, then, finding that he gets to the point of exaggerating this movement, he goes to the other extreme, club-head first, to restore a balance. Of the many ways of starting the back swing the hands-first method was the most popular, and the one recommended. This method has now been superseded by the " all-in-one-piece " movement, so popular with the Americans. We do not propose to discuss the many ways of starting the back swing. There is no finality. We recommend the all-in-one-piece method as the safest. If the beginner adopts the hands-first method, there will always be a tendency to lift the club instead of dragging it back. The all-in-one-piece movement cuts out that tendency, so common amongst beginners.

The first thing to note in starting the back swing is that the club is controlled mainly by the left arm. The left arm, being in command, should be slightly firmer than the right. This is due to the firm grip with the left hand, a firmness which is slightly intensified just as the back swing starts. We do not mean that the left arm should be stiff and rigid. The arms, hands, and club all go back together as if in one piece. This keeps the face of the club square to the ball. As the arms, hands, and club go back, there is a slight lateral movement of the hips from left to right, and simultaneously the shoulders begin to rotate. With the lateral movement of the hips the first step in transferring the weight to the right foot begins. It is very important to note that when the shoulders begin to rotate the head must not move with them. It remains fixed. If it does not, you will sway—a common fault. To obviate this, it will help you if you tilt your head slightly to the right just before starting the back swing.

The back swing must not be hurried. Remember that the greatest speed of the swing is reached at impact. Many beginners reverse the process ; their back swing is faster than their down swing. Draw the club, without hurry, straight back, and close to the ground for about twelve inches, keeping the club-face square to the ball

The body gradually keeps turning until, finally, the shoulders rotate to a position where they are at right angles to the line of direction. The head has not moved, and the chin should be just inside the top of the left shoulder. As the body turns, so should the weight be transferred to the heel of the right foot. The left knee bends slightly inwards and forward so that it is pointing towards the ball, opposite the left heel. The left heel rises only a little, and the weight of the left leg should be on the inside of the ball of the foot. Jones raised his left heel high but the leading players to-day do not : and beginners are not recommended to follow Jones's example in this particular point. Too often they have the weight of the left leg on the " toe " only, and frequently they turn the left heel outwards. Apart from the slight rise of the heel, the left foot should remain in its original position, as at the address.

The arms should be kept close to the body. When they reach about waist high on the back swing, the left arm should be straight and almost parallel to the ground ; the right arm should be slightly bent, with the right elbow close to the right side. When the club is raised from that position the wrists must bend. This bending is often called the " breaking " or " cocking " of

B

the wrists. The break should be natural, not deliberate. The club now rises vertically, and as it **is** raised so should the right arm bend till

Half-way back ; wrists about to " break ". Left knee slightly bent, with weight being gradually transferred to right foot ; left arm straight ; head does not move with rotation of shoulders.

the forearm is nearly vertical. The right elbow should be down, pointing to the ground. That **is** important. The right elbow should also have **m**oved away slightly from the side of the body.

You are recommended to keep the left arm straight, but older players may find this physically impossible at the top of the swing. There is little harm in having the left arm slightly bent at this stage, but it should not remain bent. If it is bent, it should straighten soon after the down swing has started. The club at the top of the swing is approximately parallel to the ground. In this respect the best players differ slightly. Some, like Ben Hogan, take the club further back ; others, like Cotton, not so far. Take the club back just as far as you can control it without losing balance. At the top of the swing the shoulders should have turned about 90 degrees, the hips about half as much, from the start of the back swing. Your grip on the club, particularly with the left hand, must not be relaxed at the top of the swing. That is very important.

Before beginning the down swing some players make an almost imperceptible pause. Byron Nelson says that " the way to ensure good timing in your swing is to slow down your back swing to a point of slight hesitation at the top ". We agree, but we think he will mislead many of his readers when he adds, " Motion of body, arms, hands, and club must all stop at top before down swing is started." The pause is so slight that it is almost imperceptible ; there must be no dead stop, otherwise all rhythm would be lost. Body action, says Ben Hogan, plays an important part

Top of the swing, straight left arm, right elbow pointing to the ground, firm grip with left hand, most weight on right heel. Note head position.

in the golf swing when the body turns as fast as possible from the top of the swing to the left. " Don't stop your body," he continues, " once you have initiated the swing. Keep it moving throughout if you want to develop power." Whatever you do, don't make a distinct pause.

Just as the first movement of the back swing is a lateral movement of the hips from left to right, so the first movement in the down swing is a lateral movement of the hips from right to left, the reverse process. The lateral movement of the hips on the down swing, however, is much quicker than the corresponding movement on the back swing. This is the first step in transferring the weight from the right foot to the left. The shoulders, arms, and hands follow the hip movement. Most beginners reverse the process and start the club down with the hands. The result is they " uncock " their wrists too soon, and thereby lose much of their power. The hip movement almost automatically starts the shoulders, arms, hands, and club on the down swing. Just as the left arm dominates on the back swing, so does it take command on the down swing. There is a natural tendency to let the right dominate the left. Keep the arms close to the body, with the right elbow well into the right side of the body. The down swing is gradually accelerated until it reaches its maximum speed at impact. The hands do not begin to unleash their power until they come into what is called " the hitting area ", approximately the last quarter of the downward arc. It is at this point the right hand comes into play, when the wrists begin to " uncock ". At impact both hands release all the power that was stored up in the cocking of the wrists ; and both hands should have returned to the position in which they were at the address.

As the down swing gets on its way, the weight of the body is mostly transferred to the left foot. At impact the left foot should be firmly planted on the ground with the left leg and left side well braced. The act of transferring the weight to the left foot is assisted by an inward thrust of the right foot when the hands come into the hitting area. This thrust of the right foot causes the right knee to bend and the right heel to rise. Ben Hogan maintains that this thrust or shove with the right foot, as the club-head approaches the ball, gives him extra distance with his woods and long irons. It is also interesting to note that in addressing the ball he exerts some pressure with the inside of his right foot.

Let the club-head follow through to the natural completion of the down swing. The arms pull the shoulders round till the body is facing the line of play. At the completion of the follow-through nearly all the weight of the body is on the outside of the left foot.

Finish of swing. Left leg well braced with weight on left foot. Grip with both hands still firm.

All the movements producing a free, full, rhythmic swing should merge into one ; they should not appear to be separate or distinct.

II. The Brassie

Nearly all that has been said of the driver is applicable to the brassie. The face of the brassie has a little more loft than that of the driver, which has little or no loft. The reason for this is simple : the brassie is used for long shots played from the fairway ; and the slight loft really takes the place of the tee used with the driver.

It must be emphasized that the brassie should be used only when the lie of the ball is favourable. If the ball is " cupped " or lying very close, a spoon should be used. In certain circumstances the experts can and do use a brassie from such a lie, just as they can use a driver from a favourable lie on the fairway, when extra distance is required.

The stance with the brassie is the same as that with the driver, provided both clubs are " matched ". The ball at the address should be slightly further back than it is with the driver, so that the hands are in line with the ball, and not behind it as with the driver. Swing as with the driver, but try to let the club-head graze or just skin the turf. This skinning of the turf, combined with the loft on the face of the brassie,

Brassie, the address, hands in line with ball, otherwise
same as driver.

should make the ball rise and fly with the trajectory required, provided the ball is properly struck.

III. The Spoon

Of all the clubs in a set, the spoon is one of the most useful. In length it is a little shorter than the brassie, and the face has a little more loft. The extra loft on the face of the spoon gives the beginner and high-handicap player more confidence ; he realizes that it should be comparatively easy to get the ball up without any special effort on his part.

The ball at the address should be a little further back than it is with the brassie so that the hands are slightly ahead of the ball. The object of this is to bring about the more effective operation of the loft on the face of the club. The ball should rise fairly quickly, and stop soon after it has hit the ground.   The spoon is thus very useful when a high shot to the green is required.   The ordinary player who is not sufficiently expert to make a long iron shot stop quickly will find it easier to use a spoon instead. All he has to do is to adopt an open stance and grip the spoon a little further down the shaft.

The spoon is also most useful for playing shots from a " cuppy " or close lie, or from a hanging or downhill lie. It can also be used effectively from a reasonably good lie in the semi-rough, provided distance is required.   If distance is not to be of any advantage, it is better to sacrifice a few yards and place your shot so that the next stroke will be comparatively easy. Too many players do not think ahead. Golf is like billiards in that you must try to leave yourself in the most favourable position for the next stroke.

In playing a spoon from a " cuppy " lie, do not try to sweep the ball away. Hit down and through the ball, as it were, skinning the turf immediately in front of the ball. Hit the bag first, then the turf. The squeezing or pinchinll of the ball between the club-face and the turf makes the ball rise. If you try to sweep the ball away from a " cuppy " lie you will probably hit the ground immediately behind the ball, making a " sclaffed " or topped shot.

CHAPTER V

THE LONG IRONS

(Nos. 1, 2, 3)

IRON play differs from wood club play in that a greater degree of accuracy is required with irons. Direction is not the only essential; range is equally important. A drive can generally finish with impunity anywhere on the fairway, to the right, or left, or in the middle; it may travel further than, or not as far as, we expected. With iron shots there is less scope. A slight inaccuracy in direction or range is more likely to find some kind of trouble, especially when the green is well guarded by hazards.

Except in special circumstances, the roll or run of the ball should be restricted; with wood shots there is no such necessity, except perhaps with the spoon. The run of the ball is restricted by means of back-spin. To produce back-spin, iron shots must be played with more of a descending blow than wood shots. To facilitate this it is customary to play the ball a little further back, about midway between the feet—not opposite

Address ; long iron ; arms closer to body than with " woods ".

the left heel as with the driver. Theoretically this is sound advice, but with the ball in this position the ordinary player often produces a low shot to the right, as a result of hitting the ball near the heel of the club. An inch or so either way in the position of the ball may make a considerable difference, and it is well worth while to experiment and find which position gives the best results. The same applies to wooden clubs. Irons are shorter than woods, consequently we must stand nearer to the ball. Do not bend over the ball ; stand erect, bending the knees slightly to avoid rigidity ; and use a square stance. The swing for the long irons is similar to that for woods, with only slight modifications. Again, as irons are shorter than woods, the swing is a little more upright and generally not quite so full as with woods. Accuracy both in range and in direction is the key-note of all successful iron play, and to obtain this accuracy it is advisable to curtail the back swing slightly, if the back swing with woods is full and free. Those whose back swing is not so full (generally known as a three-quarter swing) do not need to restrict their swing. The grip is slightly firmer. As the descending blow with any iron cuts, as it were, first through the ball, then into the turf, it is essential to keep a firm grip so that the club-head will not turn when it cuts into the turf. The firm, descending blow prevents the ball from rolling too far by producing the desired back-spin, which, in turn, helps to steady and control the flight of the ball. The ball is pinched or squeezed between the club-face and the ground. The left arm must be firm and straight at impact ; and remember to " stay down to the shot ". In other words, keep the left shoulder, left hand, and club head down as long as possible. Many players, in attempting to get the ball up, jerk the left shoulder up at impact, thus throwing too much weight on the right foot. Let the arms and hands do the work ; and do not dip the right shoulder on the down swing.

With iron clubs particularly, it is better to use one with which the distance can be reached comfortably. In other words, " play within yourself ". Do not force with a club which may just get the distance. Forcing a long iron, or any other iron for that matter, generally results in a pulled or pushed shot ; the shot is mistimed. This is a common fault with promising young players. They like to brag that they reached such and such a green with a drive and a niblick. When they get older and more experienced, they will learn sense. The game is difficult enough without making it more so. They are also particularly prone to under-club against the wind. For example, they will force a No. 2 iron when a controlled spoon or brassie shot would be more effective.

Medium iron ; top of swing ; not so full as with " woods " ;
straight left arm ; hands high ; firm grip with both hands.
Hands head high more suitable for less supple players.

Long iron ; beginning of down swing ; weight transferred **to**
left foot ; wrists still " cocked ".

That the choice of the right club to use is sometimes difficult is illustrated by the following incident described to the writer by the late Bob Winton, a well-known club maker in Montrose. Sandy Herd, many years ago, was playing at Carnoustie and had Andrew Kirkaldy as his caddie. As Herd was approaching his ball about to play his second shot, Kirkaldy handed him his brassie. " Give me my cleek, Andra," said Sandy, " I haven't a very good stance." " Play your brassie," brusquely retorted Kirkaldy. " You play this game wi' yer heid, no' yer feet." Not knowing the full situation, one cannot pass a verdict whether Kirkaldy was correct in the choice of club, but there can be no dubiety about " You play this game wi' yer heid."

After playing an exhibition game with Vardon, the writer was somewhat surprised to hear the champion say, in a conversation after the match, that he did not mind being outdriven—he seldom was—because though he knew, for example, that with his next shot he could reach the green with his cleek, he sometimes deliberately used his brassie. He did so to mislead his opponent, or put him in a quandary as to which club to play. Vardon would grip the club a little further down the shaft, and play the shot with a slight " cut " to decrease the length of the shot. Incidentally, there never was a more accurate brassie player than Vardon. On occasion Hogan allows his

opponent to outdrive him at a short par four hole
so that he can play his second before his opponent.
He then tries to place his second shot as close as
possible to the pin. If he succeeds in laying it
close to the pin, he makes it harder for his
opponent to do likewise ; the reason of course is
purely psychological.

The modern tendency is to use irons for their
maximum range only. This we consider to be
unnecessary, unless under exceptional circumstances, for it increases the margin of error, and is
an unnecessary waste of energy.

Again, how often do we see a long-handicap
player use an iron against the wind from the tee
at a comparatively short hole, when, actually,
he could scarcely reach it with his driver. He
seems to think, because it is a short hole, it is the
right thing to do. He not only fails to appreciate
his limitations but under-estimates the effect of
the wind. A green that can be reached normally
with a No. 3 iron can, at times, be reached only
with a driver. It is only to be expected that
beginners should have comparatively little knowledge of the range of the various clubs ; experience
and practice alone will teach them.

The No. 1 iron is rarely used ; it is seldom
included in a set. The reason is that it is a very
difficult club to play, due to its having very little
loft. This means that it can be played only
when the lie of the ball is very favourable, or from

Down swing "Hitting area". Note position of head—well behind ball; inward thrust of right foot; wrists "uncocked", and hands coming into position as at address.

a tee. In the hands of an expert it can be used effectively for long, low-flying shots, particularly against the wind. If a spoon were used there would be less chance of " cheating the wind ", as the ball would tend to soar. When a No. 1 iron is not in the set, the club to be used is the spoon or the No. 2 iron. If in doubt whether the objective can be reached with a No. 2 iron, it is better to use a spoon, gripping it slightly further down the shaft. This will eradicate any doubt about " getting there ", as there will be no need to force the shot. The proper mental attitude is just as important as the proper execution of the shot. If there is any doubt in the mind before playing the shot it will persist throughout the execution, and it will certainly have an adverse effect. As all shots are not hit perfectly, the shot with the stronger club has much more chance of reaching its objective.

The No. 3 iron, with its greater degree of loft, is easier to play than the No. 1 or No. 2 iron. It is also more useful in that a greater variety of strokes can be played with it. It can be used for little shots from just off the green or for a longer run-up, and for a half-shot. The No. 4 iron is generally used for the run-up, but if the No. 3 iron is held well down the shaft it will serve equally well. The term " half-shot " is really a misnomer. It implies a half-swing, and that the ball travels half the distance of a full shot. It is

Low shot, the address, hands in front of ball, ball opposite right heel.

neither : the swing is more than half, and the ball travels, consequently, much more than half the distance of a full shot. A half-shot with a No. 3 iron can be very effective against the wind. To play this shot, turn the body slightly towards the hole, and play the ball a little further back, that is, nearer the right foot, and with the right foot at right angles to the line of play, not pointing outwards as in the normal stance. In the back swing the left arm is kept straight, almost parallel to the ground, and the right elbow is well into the right side. The wrists then " break ", and with the hands in this position the club passes a little beyond the vertical ; it has reached the limit of the back swing. The downward blow must be firm ; there must be no slackness or " letting up " to reduce the length of the shot. Keep a firm grip throughout, and stay down to the shot. At the finish of the stroke, both arms will be fully extended, almost parallel to the ground and pointing towards the objective. This shot is sometimes called a " push shot ", probably due to the position of the arms at the finish of the restricted follow-through ; the arms appear to have " pushed " the club through. If properly played, the ball will start low, then rise, and fall with little or no run—the result of the hands being kept low throughout, the position of the ball at the address (nearer the right foot), the firm decisive blow, and the effect of the head wind.

Long iron, follow-through, hands high, left leg braced.
Note position of elbows, perfect poise.

Accuracy with irons and the ability to vary their use according to conditions mark the difference between the experts and the less skilful. Some amateurs can drive as far as the leading professionals but few are as expert with irons. This fact was no doubt in the mind of Andrew Kirkaldy when he remarked, " Any d——d fool can drive."

CHAPTER VI

APPROACH SHOTS

Short Approaches

I. The Run-up Shot

THIS shot is played under certain conditions from just off the green up to about 30 yards. It must not be confused with the pitch-and-run, a longer shot that will be described later. From just off the green the run-up is very similar to an approach putt. As the ball is meant to run most of the way to the hole, it is obvious that an iron with little loft is required. Indeed, some players use a putter for this stroke, treating it just as another long putt. At St. Andrews the writer often saw the wooden putter used very effectively for the run-up by such players as Andrew Kirkaldy, Willie Greig, and James Anderson. Some players, particularly on seaside courses, prefer to use a putter, especially in the summer when the intervening ground is dry and suitable. It would be wiser policy for many ordinary golfers to do so than to jab at the ball with a No. 7 iron, as many of them do. When an iron with little loft is used from just off the green, the ball, owing to the slight loft on the iron used, will land just on the green and run all the rest of the way. This shot differs from the chip in that the ball is made to run most of the way. The run-up shot for longer distances, say, up to 30 yards, does not land on the green like one from just off the green. As the ball has to run over part of the fairway before it reaches the green, the run-up shot can be played only when the intervening ground is not likely to kill the shot or kick it off the line. If it is likely to do so, a pitch shot will be more effective. As J. H. Taylor said, " There are no hazards in the air."

In the run-up, the feet, as in all short shots, should be close together without actually touching. The stance is slightly open with the body turned a little towards the hole. To keep the ball low and running most of the way these points must be remembered. First, the ball is played at a point nearly opposite the right heel, with the hands ahead of the club-head ; secondly, the club is taken back with the left arm without " breaking " the left wrist ; and, thirdly, the club should be kept low in the back swing and then swept through the ball, still keeping the club low in the follow-through. At the finish of a long run-up both arms will be fully extended. The right wrist may tend to roll over the left at the finish but, if so, there is no need to check it as nothing then can affect the stroke.

II. The Chip Shot

The chip shot is another very short approach shot. It is unlike the longer run-up in that the ball from anywhere close to the green is " chipped " or pitched on to the green with just sufficient run to reach the hole. The club to be used will depend in normal circumstances on the distance between the edge of the green and the hole. It will be the one which, without imparting spin, will loft the ball comfortably on to the green. If the green is slow, or if the hole is at the far edge of the green, a No. 7 iron will probably suffice. Like the run-up shot, it is played with a slightly open stance and with the feet fairly close. But unlike the run-up, the stroke is played with the ball opposite a point approximately midway between the feet, and the club is not kept so low in the back swing. On the other hand, if the green is fast, or the hole is on the near edge of the green, a No. 9 iron may have to be used. If so, the ball will be played at a point nearly opposite the left heel, again with an open stance and the feet fairly close. The club-face should be laid back a little. To prevent the ball running too far some back-spin must be imparted. To do so the club should be lifted up rather sharply with a free wrist action in the back swing, thus bringing about a steeper descending blow. But do not take the club up with the wrists alone as

Address for chip. Ball midway between feet, feet close, hands
close to body and in front of ball, head directly **over** ball,
club-head slightly laid back.

Follow-through, chip shot, head down, slight " give " in right knee, back of left hand facing hole, club face square to line of direction.

no shot in golf is purely a wrist stroke. To get this freer wrist action, grip the club less firmly but not loosely. It is very important to hit down and through the ball, and to follow through in line with the hole. If there is no follow-through, the stroke will be merely a jab.

For the little shots from just off the green it is safer to use a No. 4 or a No. 5 iron, but practice with the Nos. 7, 8, and 9 is also essential, for on occasion, owing to the contour and state of the ground, you will find that the loft on a No. 4 or No. 5 iron is not sufficient to prevent the ball from rolling across the green. It is well to remember that many little chip shots have to be played from " cuppy " lies near the green. The majority of players either half-top or fluff this shot. First, choose the club which will produce the height required ; secondly, see that the hands are slightly ahead of the ball at the address ; and, finally, hit down on the back of the ball.

III. The Pitch Shot

The pitch is a longer approach than the run-up or the chip. Much that has been said about the chip with a No. 7 iron is applicable to the pitch. For the shorter pitches the Nos. 7, 8, and 9 may be used, and the Nos. 6 and 5 for the longer ones. The No. 7 is one of the most useful of the pitching clubs, and its mastery can save many strokes. Accuracy with this club can often roll three strokes into two. In other words, if the ball is pitched reasonably close to the hole there is a chance of getting down with one putt. It used to be said that the man who could pitch did not need to putt, the inference being that he need never take more than two putts as a result of his pitching close to the flag. Nowadays, however, the best players are not content with an average of two putts per green. Our professionals agree that it is this rolling of three strokes into two from a distance of 100 yards or even more that gives the American professionals their supremacy. The pitch is not only one of the most effective shots in golf but it is the prettiest to watch. To see the ball pitched high in the air covering the flag and dropping " dead " provides one of the finest thrills in golf. This is the stroke that seems to mystify the long-handicap player, yet, to the expert, it is one of the easiest and most delightful strokes to play.

How is it played ? First, study the following preliminaries : open stance with feet fairly close ; knees slightly bent forward ; arms close to the body ; the body slightly turned towards the hole ; the ball opposite a point approximately midway between the feet ; grip firmly with the left hand and thumb and forefinger of the right hand ; hands slightly in front of club-head ; lay the club-head back a little or, in other words, " open " the face to increase the loft.

And now the stage is set for the execution of the shot. Take the club back with the left arm in command ; keep the left arm close to the body so that the straight left arm and the club are almost in a straight line. The left heel at this point will just be off the ground, if at all, as some of the weight has been transferred to the right foot, though there should be considerable pressure on the ball of the left foot. The pull of the left arm brings round the left shoulder considerably but there is very little hip movement. At this point it is important to see that the right elbow is close to the right side. After reaching this point the wrists are sharply " cocked " and the club rises almost vertical with the left arm still straight and the right elbow close to the side. From this position the arms are slightly raised by the full cocking of the wrists till the hands are level with the right shoulder. There is no need to take the club any further back. Having reached the top of the swing, note the following points : the grip with the left hand should still be firm, and the thumb and forefinger of the right hand should be squeezing the grip ; there should be a feeling of complete command over the club ; the weight of the body should be on the heel of the right foot and the ball of the left foot ; the heel of the left foot is only slightly raised at the top of the back swing. Before the start of the down swing there should be a slight pause, so

C

slight that it is almost imperceptible. This pause has a steadying effect preparatory to the downward blow and gives the eye time to fix on that part of the ball which is to be hit. In the upward swing there has been a considerable turn of the shoulders, so in the down swing the left arm and left shoulder bring the club down and the shoulders round to their original positions, as at the address. Keep the left arm straight and both arms close to the body. As the club descends, the left heel is firmly clamped to the ground with the transfer of weight to the left side. The wrists are not fully uncocked till impact. At this point the grip with both hands must be firm and the left arm straight, with the back of the left hand facing towards the line of play. The down swing must be a firm, decisive blow, as the harder you hit into the ball the more back-spin will be imparted by hitting first into the ball, then into the turf. By this means the ball is firmly squeezed against the turf by the face of the club, and this produces the desired back-spin. One final warning in playing this shot : keep the head down and as steady as possible. In this shot there is a great tendency to raise the head immediately the ball is struck. Hit down and follow through, remembering that the follow-through is not so long as that of the longer clubs. If you practise this stroke, perhaps the most important of all and certainly the prettiest, you will find that by diligent and

No. 7 iron ; finish of full shot. Don't forget to follow **through ;** follow-through **is not so** full as with " woods ".

intelligent practice you will reduce your score by several strokes.

IV. The very short pitch over a bunker or natural feature

This is generally admitted to be one of the most difficult shots in golf. Even though modern clubs, particularly American, have been produced for this particular type of stroke, the shot is still a difficult one to master completely, especially if the hole is on the near side of the green, or if the green is fast. Even from a good lie it is not an easy shot, but from a " cuppy " or hanging lie it is still more difficult. Much of the difficulty is increased by the mental attitude. The player's mind is obsessed : his mental troubles are concerned with the bunker immediately in front, the nearness of the hole to the bunker, and how to get sufficient back-spin to prevent the ball from rolling across the green. While actually playing the shot he is thinking of one or of all these things instead of concentrating on hitting the ball properly to get the result desired. As the distance is so short, the common tendency is to make a short, sharp jab in an attempt to produce the necessary back-spin. The result nine times out of ten is that the ball and a divot slowly but surely follow each other into the bunker. It is obvious that to play this shot a considerable amount of back-spin is required, so choose the

club with the biggest loft. Stand with the feet
fairly close using an open stance, and play the
ball from a point approximately opposite the left
heel. Take a slightly shorter grip of the club,
but don't crouch. The hands at the address
should be just a little above the knees. Visualize
the stroke you want to play, and try to dismiss the
bunker from your mind entirely. We have
previously stated that no golf stroke is made by
wrist action only. This particular shot is played
with the wrists and forearms. As it is a delicate
little shot, accurate hitting is essential. The
playing of this shot differs from the normal pitch
shot in that the club, to permit freer wrist action,
is not held so firmly. The back swing should
be very upright, slower, and fairly long despite
the short distance between the ball and the hole.
The eyes should be directly above the ball and
the head should be kept steady. As the stroke is
played with the forearms and wrists there is
practically no body movement. At impact the
wrists should be fully uncocked and the left arm
straight, with the back of the left hand facing the
line of play. The ball is struck a sharp downward blow with a flick of the wrists at impact.
Allow the club to follow through on the line of
play so that the stroke will not be a jab at the
ball.

As the stroke is played with little or no body
movement, one would imagine that it should be

comparatively easy to keep the head steady, but it is a fact that many players, in their anxiety to see the result of the stroke, lift the head too soon. Try to keep the head steady, and keep it down till the shot is well on its way. The head is too often raised at impact, and the result is usually disastrous. When you address the ball for this particular shot it is a good thing to remind yourself to keep the head down. Keep your head down, don't hurry the swing, relax by not gripping the club too firmly so as to give the wrists and forearms free play. And, finally, forget about that intervening bunker.

V. The Pitch with the Mashie (No. 5 and No. 6 irons)

When the range of the approach shot is beyond the power of the No. 7 iron, a No. 6 or a No. 5 iron must be used. The No. 5 iron can also be used effectively for the chip and pitch-and-run shot. The No. 6, with its slightly more lofted face, is also useful on occasion for playing approach shots out of the semi-rough or from a very favourable lie in a bunker when some distance is required.

The stance for the No. 5 and No. 6 irons is the same, slightly open. The same stance is used for the No. 4. The ball is played opposite a point approximately midway between the feet ; and at the address the hands are slightly ahead of the

No. 5 iron; address; slightly open stance; ball nearly midway between feet; weight equally distributed between
both feet; arms close to body.

club-head. Stand fairly erect without any semblance of stiffness. To do this, bend the knees slightly. Take a firm grip of the club with the left hand and thumb and forefinger of the right. The club is taken back with the left arm and is kept straight and close to the body. The right elbow should be kept close to the side but not quite so close as with the No. 7, as the back swing is not quite so upright. There is also more lateral shifting of the hips with the No. 5 than with the No. 7. When the club is taken back, the right leg should straighten, with some of the weight transferred to the right heel. At the same time the left knee bends slightly inwards. The left heel is slightly raised, and considerable weight is put on the ball of the left foot. With the bending of the left knee, take care not to allow the body to lean forward. As with the No. 7, there is no need to take the club back higher than the point where the hands are level with the right shoulder. The downward blow is not so steep as with the No. 7 but otherwise the action is similar. It will be as well to recall these points. At impact the left heel must be firmly anchored to the ground ; the left leg and the left arm must be straight, with the back of the left hand to the line of play. Follow through after impact, keeping the club as low to the ground as long as possible. Do not sweep the ball off the ground. Hit it a decisive, downward blow. If the ball is swept away there will be no " bite " in the shot, and there will be less control over its flight. If you are getting too much run on your approach shots, you may be hitting the ball up after the club has reached the bottom of the arc. In other words, you have hit the ball a fraction of a second too late. The ball should be hit at the bottom of the downward swing and not afterwards. Again, at impact, you may have too much weight on your right foot. The weight has not been sufficiently or timeously transferred to the left side. The left side must be braced at impact, with the left foot firm on the ground. Remember that the ball must be pinched or squeezed against the turf by the club-face. Do not " delve " at the ball, taking the turf first. Hit into and through the ball, as it were, and then the turf will be cut just in front of where the ball lay, and not behind it.

VI. The Pitch-and-Run Shot

Under certain conditions the pitch-and-run is most useful. It can be effectively employed on seaside courses when in summer the ground is hard and dry, or in winter when the ground is frozen. Under these conditions, when the greens are fast it is well-nigh impossible to pitch the ball on to the green and stop it there. The stroke, as the name implies, is a combination of pitch and run. There is no need to open the stance, though some prefer a slightly open stance. The ball can be played from opposite a point midway between the feet or preferably a little further back, nearly opposite the right heel. The club is taken back with a straight left arm. It is kept low not only in the back swing but in the follow-through as well. The idea of keeping the club low both ways is to impart over-spin to the ball and to make it run as truly as the ground will permit. The ball in this shot runs much further than the chip or the pitch shot. To get plenty of run some players allow the right hand to roll over the left at impact, but this action can lead to trouble if not properly timed. The pitch-and-run is usually played with the No. 4 or No. 5 iron. It is used when a pitch is out of the question owing to dry, fast ground, or a following wind or both. When the greens are " holding ", a pitch is preferable as there are no hazards in the air. A well-played pitch-and-run shot may be harshly treated by the intervening ground, but that risk on occasion must be taken. The " breaks " may be with or against you.

There is little distinction between the longer run-up and the pitch-and-run shot. The run-up is played from just off the green and up to about thirty yards. Beyond that and up to twice that distance either a pitch-and-run or a pitch shot can be played, according to the conditions already described.

VII. The Sand-Wedge Pitch : an American method

A noticeable feature in Ben Hogan's recently published book, *Power Golf*, is the omission of the Run-up and the Pitch-and-Run. Hogan at the time of publication had never played in this country. When Jones came to this country he soon found that, if he were to master the conditions prevailing on our seaside courses particularly, he had to learn how to play these shots. As the greens in America are well soaked with water, it is comparatively easy to pitch on to the green, and there is, consequently, no necessity to play the run-up. The Americans favour the more spectacular pitch. But the greatest virtue of the run-up is that, as Jones says, it will never finish very far away from the hole.

" If there is one club in the bag neglected by novices and duffers," says Hogan, " it is the sand-wedge." The sand-wedge, according to him, is not used for bunkers only ; he maintains that it is ideal for pitch shots because of its loft, and the wide flange on the sole of the club which prevents the blade from digging into the ground. It is ideal when you want the ball to stop quickly after it lands. Hogan even goes so far as to state that if anyone will take the trouble to learn how to use it, the sand-wedge can be the most useful club in the kit. All you have to do, according to him, is " to hit a little back of the ball ". He advises his readers to use this club " for all pitch shots from your maximum distance right on in to the green ".

Hogan obviously attributes much of his success to his use of the sand-wedge. After much practice he has perfected this shot, suitable for conditions in America. It is questionable, however, if he would use this club for all his pitches in the conditions prevailing here. We believe that it is safer for the ordinary player in this country to play the run-up and the pitch-and-run when the conditions are favourable for these shots. The run-up, as we have stated, will not finish far away from the hole, but we can visualize the ball scampering over the green if the front edge of the sole of the wedge connects with the ball. The wedge shot demands more precise hitting. That the sand-wedge is a most useful club cannot be denied ; and its usefulness is not confined to bunkers.

CHAPTER VII

PUTTING

IF you watch the leading players putt, you will find that the majority stand with their feet fairly close together. This is to be expected, as it is a general rule that the shorter the stroke the closer the feet. The right foot is generally a little in advance of the left, though the square stance and the closed stance can also be successfully adopted. In putting, most of the weight is placed on the left foot. There should be no feeling of rigidity or stiffness in the legs or body. One must feel comfortable. Both arms are slightly bent, the left perhaps a little more so than the right. The left elbow should be pointing towards the line of play. The right elbow is tucked close to the body and rests very lightly on the corresponding thigh. The body should be held fairly erect without being stiff. The head is bent forward and should be directly above the ball in any normal stance. The head, body, and legs, for shorter putts at least, should be kept perfectly steady while the hands, wrists, and forearms are in action. The head should be kept down until the follow-through is completed.

Body erect, knees slightly bent, slightly open stance, ball opposite left toe, arms slightly bent and close to body, head directly over ball. Note position of hands—against shaft ; comfortable position, without any tension of body, legs, and arms.

The hands play a very important part in putting. No stroke requires more delicacy or " touch ". It is in this part of the game that the first-class American golfers are supreme. Various reasons are given : the well-watered and consistent greens in America, it is alleged, give the Americans confidence to putt boldly. There is only a modicum of truth in this, for no matter what the condition of the greens, fast or slow, the Americans remain supreme. Another reason put forward is that the Americans practise more. This is true, but it is not the whole truth. It contains the secret : their practice is diligent and intelligent. They practise hard ; they experiment ; they know exactly what they want to do and how to do it ; and they remember how to do it.

The writer once asked a leading English professional what method he adopted when putting. He confessed that he did not know. How different when the same question was put separately to two famous Americans. One instantly replied, " Back with the left, through with the right." The method used by his compatriot was quite different. He used his right ; in other words, the right hand was dominant throughout the putting stroke. It so happened that the English professional just mentioned won the Open Championship the following year, mainly due to good putting. It would be wrong to deduce from this that it is better not to know how you execute a particular stroke. It would be interesting to know whether this professional in the interval learned wisdom. Unless you know what you are doing, or not doing, you cannot correct any fault that may arise. You must be able to "check up".

The importance of the hands has been stressed. Yet it must be admitted that in putting one cannot be dogmatic about their use. The best putters agree to differ as to the method to be used. Let us consider the different methods employed by the aforementioned Americans. First, " back with the left, through with the right". This is self-explanatory : the left hand takes command as the putter is drawn back, then the right takes over in completing the forward stroke. Secondly, " all right hand ". This does not mean that the left hand plays no part ; it simply means that the right hand is dominant throughout. Of these two methods the second seems less complicated, yet, as it happened, the professional who adopted the first method was the better putter. In fact, he was then recognized as the best putter in America. Though this method obviously suited him, it does not follow that it must be adopted by all. It is better than the other in one respect at least : there is less tendency to lift the putter too high on the back swing.

But it can be maintained, and maintained successfully, that neither hand should be the

master at any time. In other words, both hands
should work together as one. At all events there
must be unison. When you are putting well you
will find that this is so. You will not be con-
scious of the mastery of either hand. Experiment, and if you find a better method, by all
means adopt it.

The grip on the putter differs slightly from that
on the other clubs. Take the left hand first.
It should not be placed so far over the shaft ;
the back of the hand should be at right angles to
the line of play. The thumb is placed down the
shaft, not diagonally across it. Grip the putter
firmly with the last three fingers. In the ordinary
grip you see two knuckles at least of your left
hand, but with this grip you will see none. This
is the grip generally adopted by those who take
the putter back with the left hand. The right
hand, too, is not so far over the shaft, and the
thumb generally points more down the shaft.
Those who maintain that they putt with the
right hand as master, generally grip the putter
firmly with the thumb and forefinger of the right
hand. They also hold the putter fairly firmly
with the last three fingers of the left hand ; and
the position of both hands is generally as just
described. Both hands must be close together,
using an over-lapping or interlocking grip according to preference.

The main object is to put the ball into the

hole no matter what method is adopted. It is of the utmost importance to take the putter back properly. If it is not, then it is unlikely that the ball will be struck accurately with the blade of the putter square to the ball. There is a natural tendency to take the putter back off the line away from the body. The result is that the putter is brought forward with its face not square to the ball at impact. This inaccuracy will be aggravated in the longer putts, as the longer the putt the longer the back swing. The putter should be taken straight back, not away from the body. To take the putter back smoothly and accurately is not as easy as one would imagine. It requires constant practice. If you succeed, half the battle is over. You will form a good idea whether your putt is to be successful or not when you are on the back swing. Any attempt to correct it in the forward movement will likely prove disastrous. The final, smooth, and all-important stroke must be made with a firm left wrist. There should be no jabbing.

The putter should be held neither too tightly nor too slackly. If the putter is held tightly the muscles of the wrists and forearms become too tense and prevent free movement of the hands. If it is held too slackly there is every chance of losing some control over the putter, thereby destroying some of the rhythm of the stroke ; it will look like a half-hearted effort.

Back swing for longish putt, no wrist " break ", club-face
as square as possible to line of direction.

The head or blade of the putter should be kept low not only on the back swing but in the follow-through. The length of the back swing and the follow-through varies according to the length of the putt. Only practice will teach you how far to take the putter either way. At times you may find that there is a tendency for the right hand to roll over the left resulting in the ball finishing to the left of its objective. It is to counteract this that the left hand is held not so far over the shaft. In fact, both hands are held more against the shaft than over it, both hands counteracting each other, yet working harmoniously.

Many putts, particularly short ones, are missed through moving the head. Anxiety to see the result makes the player look too soon at the progress of the ball on its way to the hole. Again, when close to the hole, the player, instead of concentrating on the ball, sees the hole through the " tail " of his left eye ; his attention is divided and the result is usually failure. One should turn a blind eye to the hole under such circumstances. Short putts require care at all times, and particularly so when the green is fast and the hole is cut on a slope. It is probably easier to hole a putt of two yards on the flat than to hole a yard putt on a slight slope. The effect of the slope has to be judged. Suppose allowance is made for the " borrow " or bias and the ball is struck just a trifle too strongly, the bias will fail to act in

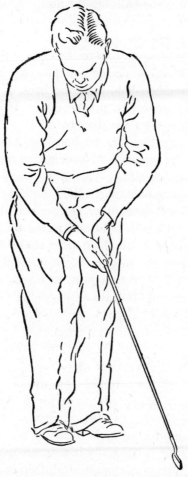

Head down, club-head low throughout entire stroke. Club-face square to line of direction

time to turn the ball into the hole. On the other hand, if the ball is not struck strongly enough, the bias will act too soon, and the ball will fade away from the hole according to the slope. Sometimes it is difficult to decide whether to make any allowance or go boldly for the back of the hole. Indecision generally proves fatal. Under such circumstances go for the hole.

There are times to be bold and times to be wary on the greens. " Never up, never in " is a well-known maxim. When the greens are slow it is wise to be bold, particularly with the holeable putts. But it is another story when the greens are fast. If one is bold and misses the hole, the ball may overrun the hole so far that it is no easy task to hole the next putt. Confidence can be shaken, and the return putt, as a result, may be struck so timidly that it fails to reach its objective. It is better to imagine, when the greens are keen, that the hole has four entrances : front, back, and two side ones. If you strike the ball with just sufficient strength it may drop in at the front entrance, or curl round the lip of the hole, dropping at either side or at the back. A ball travelling slowly has more chance of doing this. A ball running faster is likely to run over the hole, though occasionally it may hit the back of the hole, jump in the air, and drop in. It will have little chance if it hits the side of the hole.

Many spectators gasp with surprise when they see a leading player miss a short putt. They put it down to nerves or what is commonly called the " jitters ". It may be so, for nervousness will tend to make the player snatch at the ball with his putter instead of striking it smoothly. Nervousness has caused his muscles to become tense and he has lost, temporarily at least, that all-important virtue in golf, relaxation. The mind controls the nerves. It may be that the importance of the putt becomes such an obsession that he fails to think about hitting the ball correctly. A leading professional knows that one extra stroke may mean the loss of a few hundred pounds ; it may rob him of a championship. He knows that the winner's name goes down to posterity and that the runner-up, though only one stroke behind, is usually forgotten. Short putts can be missed through carelessness or over-confidence. We seem to see the ball in the hole before we have actually played, just as if holing-out were a matter of routine. The player may be disturbed by outside agencies, movement, or noise ; he may be upset by some irregularity or rough spot on the green between the hole and his ball. He may be undecided about the line, whether to borrow or not, and how much to borrow. Again, he may so concentrate on the line that his visual memory of the length of the putt fails him, and the putt usually stops short. The key to the situation is the mental attitude. When in doubt about the line, go for the hole; and if there is any rough spot in your line, forget it; hit the putt a little harder and hope for the best. Over-concentration and day-dreaming are equally fatal.

The writer has stated that the head, body, and legs should be kept still for the short putts. With the long or very long putts, sometimes called "approach-putts", they are not kept perfectly steady. The long back swing demands greater freedom and the arms come into play. To get this freer action there will be a slight lateral movement of the hips and a slight give at the knees. If this freedom is restricted the stroke will be more of a jab, especially if the wrists have mainly controlled the swing. The left arm should move forward with the stroke, keeping the head of the putter as low as possible. The forearms should come into play in all long putts. An all-wrist action has no place in long putts. In fact, it is well-nigh impossible to play an approach putt with wrist action only. Long putts and short putts are relatively more difficult than the putts of middle distance. It is difficult to gauge the distance of a long putt, as greens vary not only from course to course but often on one course. The difficulty with a short putt, say, of three feet is that it has to be hit firmly yet gently as the ball has to travel such a short distance. Short putts are often missed through trying to guide the ball gently into the hole without hitting it firmly.

All golfers, good, bad, and indifferent, should make a practice of never conceding to themselves or their opponents a putt more than a foot in length. Champions have been known to miss a putt even less than that. If the hole is on a slope, no matter how slight, even a foot putt should not be conceded. Many a short putt has been missed because a player expected his opponent to concede it. This is a trick sometimes deliberately practised. Your opponent in the early stages of the game may concede you putts up to two feet in length, then, without any apparent reason, he does not concede one which you unwarily expected. Your mental equilibrium is disturbed and the result is fatal, as a rule. It may even upset you for a few holes, especially if you missed the putt. But don't blame your opponent for lack of sportsmanship. Remember he is perfectly justified in not conceding any putt, however short, if he is so inclined. Under such circumstances never act hastily ; the reaction tends to make one do so or become tense.

In the days of the stymie * other tactics were adopted. For instance, imagine A was putting up to the hole and B's ball lay beyond at the back of the hole. A made sure that his putt was up for two reasons : never up, never in ; and if the ball overran the hole it might have stymied

* Stymie abolished 1st January 1952.

his opponent. Again, if the two balls were lying fairly close together and A putted first, he would not go for the back of the hole but would roll it up sufficiently to drop in or stay short, again shutting the door on his opponent. This was often done, especially with longer putts. These tactics were also adopted even if the balls lay apart. For instance, if A had a putt that he would be glad to lay " dead ", he rolled the ball up so that it would finish near the hole but preferably on the side of the hole from which his opponent had to putt. By so doing he might have had the fortune to stymie his opponent or made it very difficult for him to hole his putt. But if one could lay stymies deliberately from all parts of the green there would have been no need to try as it would have been easier to put the ball in the hole, which, after all, is the most important thing.

When a player misses a holeable putt and tries it over again he is generally successful. The putt seems much easier. This is such a common experience that it has given rise to a well-known and often-heard saying, " Any darned fool can do it a second time." If we relaxed over the first putt as in the second attempt we should be more successful on the green. If you are going to miss, " miss them quick ", said Alick Smith, ex-champion of America and brother of the famous Mac. But wouldn't we prefer to " hole them quick ", if we could ?

Putting is one department of the game which you can practise at home at any time you cannot get on to a putting green. Practise the swing, particularly the back swing; you can practise even without a ball. You can hit a ball if you like but it isn't likely to run truly, and the texture of a carpet is different from that of a green. The main thing is to swing the putter back and forward correctly. Watch the movement of the club head to see that it meets the ball squarely. A few minutes' practice in the winter evenings will not only keep you in touch with your putter but your putting will improve, especially if your putting action is not as good as it should be.

There are three main kinds of putters: steel, aluminium, and wooden, so-called according to the material of which the head is composed. The putter in most common use is the steel, usually one with a wry neck. Aluminium and wooden putters can be very useful for long or approach putts. They are not favoured generally for short putts, and they seem to have gone out of favour, though it must be admitted some players have used them successfully for all kinds of putts. A few players carry two putters, but there must come times when one is left in doubt as to which one is to be used. One putter in the bag is sufficient, but it is good policy to possess two, for often a change of putter works wonders, but usually only temporarily. In the final round of the Masters' Tournament at Sunningdale, in 1948, Von Nida created a sensation by returning the phenomenal score of 63 in his final round. In doing so he changed not only his putter but his putting stance. His success in the tournament was largely attributed to his remarkable putting. When Cotton won the Open Championship at Muirfield in the same year it was noted that he, too, had changed his usual putting stance ; he played the ball not opposite the toe of the left foot but further back, nearer the right foot. The experts not only practise but experiment, and adopt, for the time being at least, the methods that give them the best results.

Putting, a game within a game, lends itself to experiment more than any other part of the game. Freak putters have been invented, and there are many freak styles of putting. We have described the conventional methods, but many of the leading Americans to-day differ from the conventional. What they have tried to do is to make the " mechanics " of the putting stroke as accurate as is humanly possible. They realize that to obtain greater accuracy the head of the putter should be kept as far as possible square to the ball, as at the address, throughout the entire stroke. In the conventional stroke the face of the putter is opened on the back swing, chiefly due to " breaking " the wrists. Consequently, as the putter in the forward swing has to be brought back to its original position, as at the address, that is, at right angles to the line of direction, it must be closed just that amount it was opened in the back swing. This, obviously, demands a very

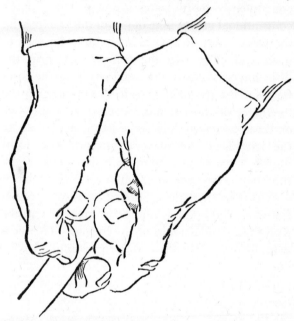

Unconventional putting grip ; reverse overlap as used by Byron Nelson ; note point of thumb.

delicate sense of timing and accuracy. Herein lies the chief source of trouble, the opening and closing of the face of the putter. To ensure greater accuracy by decreasing the possibility of error, the main object in the stroke should be, as far as possible, neither to open nor to close the face. To facilitate this, the grip has been altered. The left hand is turned slightly more to the left, and the right more to the right. Both hands are consequently more under the shaft than in the conventional grip. The object of this is to restrict the wrist action, which mainly causes the face to open and close. In the conventional grip the little finger of the right hand overlaps the forefinger of the left hand, but in the newer grip the forefinger of the left hand overlaps the last two or three fingers of the right hand, according to the length of the player's fingers. The right thumb is sometimes bent, with the point of the thumb digging into the leather.

With this grip the wrist action is very much restricted ; the hands and arms make the stroke with the shoulder joints as the hinges. The back swing is much shorter than the conventional, with no " break " of the wrists. The club is then pushed, as it were, through the ball, keeping the face of the putter square to the line of direction till the stroke is completed. The arms, wrists, and hands follow through without any bend or " break ". Even for long putts the back swing is comparatively short ; the longer the putt, the bigger the push. Herein, we think, lies the objection to this method, otherwise excellent for short or holeable putts. Those who use the conventional grip and the ordinary methods of stroking the ball will probably find that the restricted back swing and the " push " combine to upset the rhythm of the stroke for long putts ; there will be a tendency to jab. And it will be more difficult for the player to judge the strength of the putt. Patient practice, however, may overcome these difficulties. If this method is adopted, a fairly heavy, upright putter should be used.

CHAPTER VIII

BUNKER SHOTS

ONLY too soon will the beginner make acquaintance with bunkers. This is to be expected, as many of his shots are bound to go astray and find trouble. There is no need, however, to be unduly dismayed or worried when you find your ball in a sand trap, for most bunker shots are not so difficult as they appear to be.

A variety of shots can be played from bunkers, the precise shot depending on the conditions and circumstances. The first aim of the beginner should simply be to get the ball out. For him the most useful shot under any circumstances is the explosive or blast. These terms are self-explanatory. The first problem for the beginner or the expert is to judge the resistance of the sand ; it may be light, dry, and powdery, or heavy, wet, and coarse. The best way to test the sand is to " feel " with the feet as you embed them in the sand when taking your stance. This action is necessary not only to test the depth and nature of the sand but to give the feet a firm hold so that they will be less likely to slip. To avoid slipping there should be little or no pivot ; and let the arms and wrists alone do the work. This will help to prevent the feet from sinking further into the sand, particularly during a forcing shot. If the sand is wet or hard, less sand should be taken ; if it is dry and powdery, more will be taken. Experience alone will teach you where to hit the sand.

The first thing to learn is to get the ball out. Once this is accomplished, the beginner will soon learn to add to his repertoire of bunker shots. The club to use is a niblick or a sand-wedge. Adopt an open stance, with both feet well embedded in the sand. The ball should be played at a point opposite the left heel. Lay the club-head back, and aim not at the ball but at a spot fully an inch or so behind it. Precision of aim is more difficult as the rules of the game prohibit the " grounding " of the club-head in a hazard, and it is consequently by no means easy to keep the club-head absolutely steady. As quite a lot of sand will have to be dislodged in an ordinary explosive shot, a firm grip of the club should be maintained throughout to prevent the club-head from turning on impact with the sand. Don't be afraid to hit hard into the sand behind the ball. But merely to do this will only leave the ball in the bunker. The club-head must not only dig into the sand, it must plough its way through and come out of the sand. The follow-through is

D

all-important.   Do not leave the club-head buried in the sand.   This is a common fault with many golfers ; they " funk " at the last second and fail to go through on the shot, particularly from a bunker close to the green.   Being so close to the green they are afraid to hit hard ; they fail to appreciate the resistance which the club-head meets in trying to force its way through the sand. As a result they fail to get the ball out and it generally comes to rest in a worse position close to the face of the bunker.   The result will be the same if the club-head is driven too deeply into the sand or too far behind the ball.   On the other hand, if not enough sand is taken, the ball is likely to overshoot the green ; the club-head has struck the sand too near the ball.   If the sand is hard or frozen, use a niblick, not a sand-wedge ; use a sand-wedge when the sand is dry and powdery.

When the sole object is to get out of a deep-faced bunker, the easiest way out should be chosen.   Do not overlook the chance to play to either side or even backwards.   The entrance and sides are less steep as a rule.

The experts use nearly every iron for bunker shots ; it depends on the lie, the depth of the bunker, and the range required.   Do not be altogether surprised if, on occasion, you see them use the No. 4 wood.   Remember, however, that a No. 4 wood has more loft than a No. 3 iron.

But you cannot play a No. 4 wood from a bunker unless the ball is sitting up well, and provided the face of the bunker is shallow. At the best of times it is risky, as the ball has to be hit cleanly without touching the sand behind it. It is used in a more or less desperate effort when there is a possibility of reaching the green. In playing this shot there are three difficulties : the rules forbid the " grounding " of the club at the address, which, in itself, makes the shot more difficult ; the ball must be hit as clean as a whistle ; and the feet will tend to move or slip in the sand when a full shot is played. To prevent this, there should be little or no ankle pivot. The ordinary player is not likely to succeed with this shot, but there is no reason why he should not try it as an interesting experiment.

When trapped in a bunker close to the green, the expert does not rely solely on the explosive shot. He may consider that an explosive shot will not be sufficiently accurate to allow him a reasonable chance to hole out with one putt. Hagen, for example, was an expert at flicking the ball cleanly from the sand. This shot requires confidence no less than skill ; and Hagen had both in abundance. For such a shot the club to be used is one with a little more loft than would be required for the same shot to be played from the fairway. It is too dangerous and too delicate a shot for any but the expert ; the slightest error results either in a " fluff ", or the ball scampers over the green.

A less dangerous shot than the chip or flick is a modified or semi-blast stroke. It should be played with a niblick rather than a sand-wedge. The head is laid back and driven into the sand about half an inch behind the ball and just under it ; the club-head at impact is almost horizontal. As less sand has to be exploded than in the full blast, less force is applied. The stroke, however, must be as decisive and precise, with a free wrist action. It must be remembered that this stroke, like the chip from a bunker, should be employed only when the ball is lying well. If the semi-blast is properly played, the ball will rise quickly with considerable back-spin, caused by the thin layer of sand between the ball and the face of the club when it passes under the ball. Should the ball be lying in a heel-mark or foot-print, an explosive shot is the only choice.

Another bunker shot which is spectacular but dangerous is the " cut " shot. It is played with a niblick, not a sand-wedge, in the same way as the modified blast shot, except that the face of the club is drawn across the line of play from outside-in. This adds side-spin. The ball on reaching the green " breaks " sharply to the right and sometimes backwards. Leave this shot to the experts who may exploit it when the occasion demands it.

The finest cut shot from a bunker the writer ever saw was played by David Ramsay of Carnoustie, now a professional, in a tournament at Montrose. At the Long Hole his ball lay fairly close to the bank some 3 feet high and about 20 yards from the flag. He had no option but to play out sideways to the left. The ball landed on the edge of the green some 10 yards to the left of the flag, then broke sharply to the right and lay looking into the hole, laying his opponent a stymie at the same time. When the writer congratulated him on this shot, he replied, " We get plenty practice at Carnoustie." Therein lies the secret—practice and plenty of it.

Bunker shots call for originality, imagination, and daring. Bobby Jones records with much satisfaction how, at Columbus, at a critical stage in the last round of the Open Championship, he played an extremely difficult bunker shot in what might have appeared an unorthodox way. This was the situation as described by Jones. " The ball was lying near the left bank, leaving the full width of the bunker to be played over. The hole was a scant 10 or 15 feet beyond the opposite bank, and about 6 feet beyond the hole was a terrace, which would carry the ball far away down the slope if it should pass over the top of the rise." Using a mashie-iron, Jones deliberately scuttled the ball across the sand up the sloping face or bank some 2 feet high. To his great relief the ball came to rest some 4 feet from the hole, and he sank the putt. The mashie-iron has now gone out of favour ; it was a deep-faced iron with the loft of a No. 2 iron, and its length was that of a No. 4 iron.

The writer once saw his late friend, Abe Mitchell, play a disastrous, unimaginative bunker shot at Gleneagles soon after he joined the professional ranks. At " Wee Bogle " his ball lay in a very shallow bunker about 6 yards from the pin. There was no face or bank to surmount, and the ball lay cleanly on the firm sand of the gentle up-slope. Obviously about to play an explosive shot, Abe, in orthodox fashion, dug both feet well into the sand. He blasted the ball out far over the green into deep heather. He was lucky to lose only two strokes. A more imaginative player would have used a putter or a straight-faced iron. A mere tap with either would have placed the ball reasonably close for him to get down with one putt. His mental attitude may have been disturbed because he admitted to the writer that in a practice round he had found it almost impossible to get out of the deep bunker guarding the first green. The nature of the sand seemed to beat him, for less expert players found no great difficulty in getting out.

Finally, before leaving a bunker, see that you conform to the etiquette of the game by filling up any holes you may have made. You can do so with your feet or by raking the sand with your club.

Playing from the Rough

Lies in the semi-rough or rough vary, but you must consider yourself lucky if the lie is at all favourable. More often you will find the ball well bedded in the grass, probably with a tuft immediately behind the ball. In such circumstances the only thing to do is to try to dig the ball out on to the fairway, even though it may mean playing out to the side and not towards the hole. You must reconcile yourself to the fact that by so doing you are losing a stroke, but if you attempt to get greater distance you may lose a few more. And remember there is always the possibility that you may pick up the lost stroke by holing a good putt or by playing an accurate approach.

When the ball is lying deep in the grass, a club with considerable loft must be used to dig the ball out. The hands at the address should be slightly ahead of the ball. Do not open the face of the club. A firm grip must be maintained throughout so that the wrists will be firm at impact, otherwise the club-head, as it buries itself in the grass, is liable to turn. Try to hit the back of the ball hard with a rather sharp down swing. With a cushion of grass between the ball and the club-face, it is impossible to impart back-spin. As a result, there is less control over the shot, and the run of the ball, if it reaches the fairway, may be erratic.

Generally speaking, it is seldom that a club with less loft than a No. 4 iron can be played from the rough. As little or no back-spin can be imparted, remember that the ball will run further than it would if played properly from the fairway ; and it is well to remember this, parti-cularly if the green is within range. On rare occasions you may be lucky enough to get a favourable lie in the semi-rough ; if so, you may use a spoon, preferably the No. 4 wood, if distance is required. Do not use a spoon, No. 3 or No. 4 wood, as some do, if the ball is at all bedded in the grass. If you do, you will certainly play your next stroke from the rough.

CHAPTER IX

AWKWARD LIES

Uphill Lie

WHEN your drive finishes on the fairway you expect to find your ball lying reasonably well. Generally you do, but occasionally you may be unlucky. Fairways suffer from weather, wear and tear ; and few of them are absolutely flat. Your ball may come to rest in a slight depression ; or you may find that though the ball is lying well the stance is awkward. You may be even so unlucky as to find that you have, at the same time, not only an awkward stance but an uneven lie. In golf, as in all games, there is an element of luck. Two equally well-hit drives can find two very different positions on the fairway. The ability to play shots from difficult positions marks the chief difference between the experts and the less skilful players.

It is comparatively easy to play from an uphill lie, as from this position there is little difficulty in getting the ball to rise. With the left foot being higher than the right, more weight is naturally thrown on the right foot than on the left. Perfect balance is essential ; it is necessary not only for power but for what is more important, accuracy. To obtain this, the pivot should be somewhat restricted and the back swing slightly shortened. You will do this more easily if you take a shorter grip of the club.

The chief difficulty in playing from an uphill lie is to transfer the weight on to the left foot at impact. The tendency is to have too much weight on the right foot at the top of the swing, with the result that not enough weight is transferred to the left foot at impact. In the follow-through, with too much weight on the right foot, the body will tend to fall backward a little as the hands rise in the follow-through. With the weight thrown back and the right shoulder too far down one can expect almost any kind of shot— a slice, a skied shot, a top, or a " sclaff ", that is, hitting the ground behind the ball. The mis-placing of weight upsets the balance so necessary for accuracy.

It is important to remember that even if the stroke is properly executed, the ball will tend to soar, the more so if there is a head wind. To prevent the ball from rising too steeply, and to obtain consequently greater length, an expert player will use his driver rather than his brassie, if the lie is good. From an uphill lie, if you hit the ball properly, you will get a higher shot than

you would from one on the level. The higher
the flight, the less the distance, consequently you
must use a club one number lower (a club with
less loft) than you would take for the same shot
from a level lie. For example, use a brassie
instead of a spoon, remembering to take a
shorter grip. The same applies to all iron shots,
for example, a No. 4 instead of a No. 5, a No. 6
instead of a No. 7.

The ball must be played where the lowest part
of the swing will be, that is, forward towards the
left foot. Try to sweep the ball away cleanly
with the club-head following the slope. An
uphill lie tempts the beginner and the ordinary
player to have a " go ". Do not be tempted.
Hit easily, for by so doing you are less likely to
lose your balance. If you try to hit hard you
will probably overswing, lose balance and control.

It is also worth noting that, when playing from
the flat to a green which lies uphill, one should
choose a stronger club than one would use to a
green on the same level.

Downhill Lie

To play from a downhill lie is more difficult
than from one uphill. It is by no means easy to
get the ball to rise from such a lie. This is due
not only to the nature of the lie but to the fact
that more weight than usual is on the left foot,

the left foot being lower than the right. It is essential then to use a club with more loft than one would from a level lie. Stand closer to the ball, taking a slightly shorter grip ; swing a little more upright, and open the stance slightly.

The great mistake in playing this shot is to try to assist the club to raise the ball in the air. In doing so, most players strike the ground behind the ball, producing a " sclaffed " or a topped shot. Use a club with sufficient loft to raise the ball the desired height. Let the club do the work. Make no attempt to " dig " the ball up ; the club-head should follow the slope, and just skin the turf. Again, the ball must be played where the lowest part of the swing will be, that is, back, more towards the right foot.

If the slope runs not only down but towards you, the tendency will be to hook or pull ; if it runs away from you the tendency will be to push or slice. Make allowance for this by aiming a little to the right or to the left according to circumstances.

Below the ball

From such a lie the tendency is to hook. Control of the shot is the first essential. The longer the shot the more difficult it is to keep the ball from going off the straight.

First, take a slightly shorter grip of the club.

Adopt a square stance with the ball opposite a point midway between the feet. Restrict the pivot and curtail the back swing; and on no account try to force or press the shot. If you force the shot your down swing will resemble the forward sweep of a scythe, and a wild hook is likely to result. Your body will tend to turn away and back from the ball. To counteract this tendency, put a little more weight on the balls of the feet. Hit easily but firmly, and try to prevent the right hand rolling over the left too soon—the chief danger in this shot. The follow-through should be curtailed but you must play through the ball, keeping the club-head travelling on the line of direction as far as possible. A full follow-through is likely to produce a shot off the straight. Again it is advisable to sacrifice a little distance for accuracy.

Above the ball

To play a good shot from such a position is fundamentally a question of balance. One has to be careful not only when pivoting but particularly on the down swing. The natural tendency is to fall forward, as the weight is inclined to be thrown on to the toes. If the balance is upset through falling or leaning forward there will be little or no follow-through. The resulting stroke is almost certain to be unsatisfactory. Anything

Standing below ball; weight on balls of feet; shorter grip of club; ball midway between feet; square stance.

Standing above ball, knees more bent than normally; weight on heels; hands at end of grip.

may happen, but the ball generally flies off to the right, just as it often flies off to the left when one is standing below the ball.

Do not on any account try to force the shot as this will only aggravate the tendency to fall forward. It is better to sacrifice a little distance for accuracy, especially if it is impossible to reach the green. To maintain better balance it is advisable to keep the weight mostly on the heels, as this will counteract the tendency to fall forward. To make sure you will reach the ball, take a longer grip of the club. The knees should be bent more than they would normally, and instead of being erect you will assume something of a sitting position. Curtail the back swing, as this will minimize the possibility of over-balancing. The down swing and the follow-through are all-important, for it is on the down swing that balance is most likely to be upset. If you press, you are almost certain to fall forward ; you will mistime the shot and there will be little or no follow-through. Try to keep your balance by hitting easily and keeping your weight on the heels as much as possible. Stay down to the shot as long as possible ; do not raise the head and shoulders. Finally, aim slightly left to allow for a probable fade to the right.

To practise all these shots from awkward lies is time well spent.

CHAPTER X

COMMON FAULTS

Topping

EVEN the best of players make mistakes at times. When they do, it is usually on the green, or hooking or pushing the long shots. Very rarely do they completely top a shot—a very common experience with beginners and high-handicap players. Many golfers imagine wrongly, but excusably, that topping is always caused by hitting the ball on the top on the down swing. In most cases this is not so. The ball, when topped, is generally hit soon after the club-head leaves the ground on the up swing.

Topping is often the result of a too deliberate attempt to make the ball rise, an attempt which not only defeats its own ends but usually produces a result the opposite of the one intended. In an effort to get the ball up, the beginner often dips the left knee on the back swing. As a result the left shoulder is too low and the right too high at the top of the back swing. Then, on the down swing, the right shoulder is dipped and the left shoulder consequently is pulled up abruptly. Thus, throughout the swing, the arc has been raised. When this happens, the ball is hit, if at all, above the middle, and this, of course, means a topped shot. Do not try to swing the club-head under the ball. Remember that when the intention is to get the ball up quickly, it must be hit a descending blow just before the club-head

TOPPING—MORE FREQUENT ON UP SWING THAN ON DOWN SWING

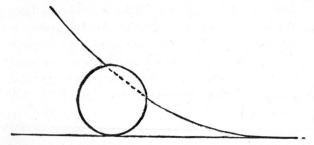

reaches the bottom of the downward arc. This applies particularly to irons.

Topping, of course, can be caused by hitting the ball above middle on the down swing. When this happens, the club has usually been lifted steeply and brought down too sharply. The result is that the ball is usually topped ; it may be " skied " if the club-head hits the ground immediately before impact and connects with the ball below the middle. Instead of swinging to the ball the player has chopped at it. The basic reason for this is that not enough weight has been transferred to the right foot on the back swing.

Raising the head or looking up too soon may also cause topping. Even good players commit this error sometimes when under strain. It is also a common experience when playing into the sun. Against the sun it is very difficult to follow the flight of the ball and, knowing this, players lift their heads too soon in an effort to get a glimpse of the ball before it goes into the sun. Keep the head down, but remember that to keep the head down too long, at least in a full shot, restricts the movement of the right shoulder. The head should turn naturally with the body when the hands are about head high in the follow-through.

The following incident illustrates how, in one case, topping was cured. A certain player, given to topping, went to George Braid, the well-known St. Andrews instructor, to get advice. " I want to see you top these balls," said George to his pupil. " Go ahead," he continued, " and don't forget I said, ' Top them '." The pupil tried his best, but to his amazement the ball always rose. Actually in trying to top the ball he was now hitting down and through the ball instead of behind it. We do not suggest that this method will cure topping but it may help in some cases.

Just as raising the arc of the swing can produce a topped shot, so can the shifting of its axis. What happens is this : the body sways to the

right on the back swing. The body, consequently, must sway to the left on the down
swing to get back to its original position.   Therein
lies the danger : the body rarely returns to the
exact position as at the address.   As the axis of
the arc has been shifted to the right, there is
every likelihood that the club-head will strike
the ground behind the ball and hit it above
middle on the up swing.   Watch, then, and see
how your back swing starts.   Avoid swaying by
not allowing your head to move with the shoulders
on the back swing.

Slicing

Slicing, that is driving the ball with a swerve
to the right, is more closely related to topping
than most golfers imagine.   We have seen that
trying to raise the ball in the air may produce a
topped shot.   It can also cause a slice.

With beginners, at least, the cause of slicing, as
with topping, can be traced, in the first instance,
to the attempt by the player to assist the club to
get the ball up in the air.   To get the ball up,
the " slicer " opens the face of the club as he hits
the ball.   In trying to raise the ball, the beginner
naturally draws his arms in towards the body on
the down swing.   He feels he has to lift his club
to make the ball rise, and it is this feeling that
causes him to pull in his arms.   It also makes

him throw the club outwards on the back swing
to give him more freedom to pull his arms in at
impact. He cuts across the ball with the face
of the club open, thus imparting a spin which
makes the ball swerve to the right. The club,
as it were, is travelling from right to left across
the ball while the club-head is facing somewhere
towards the right of the intended line of flight.

MOST COMMON CAUSE OF SLICE

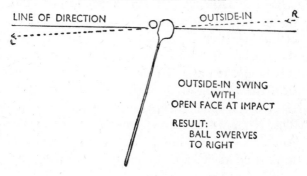

LINE OF DIRECTION   OUTSIDE-IN   R

OUTSIDE-IN SWING
WITH
OPEN FACE AT IMPACT

RESULT:
BALL SWERVES
TO RIGHT

The point to note is that the face of the club is
" open " at impact, and that drawing the club
across the ball is not in itself the cause of the
slice ; it depends on the position of the club-head
at impact. These two factors, drawing the club
across the ball, and the " open " face at impact,
are the cause of most slicing ; and the harder
the ball is hit in this way the greater the slice.
It is important then to note particularly the
position of the hands and club-head at impact,

and the direction they take immediately afterwards. There is a simple test which you can apply to see whether you draw the club-head across the ball from outside-in. Insert a peg tee about 5 or 6 inches in front of the ball and about 3 or 4 inches to the left of the intended line of direction. If you knock the tee in front out of the ground after hitting the ball, your swing is definitely from the outside-in.

To avoid slicing, it would seem obvious that the first thing for a beginner to do is to get rid of the idea that he must assist the club to raise the ball into the air. If the ball is hit properly it is bound to rise. To counteract a slice, try to send the club-head through the ball out to the right of the line, that is, away from the body. This is known as hitting from inside-out. The American experts mostly adopt this method of hitting all their shots, unless circumstances and conditions demand adjustment.

One of the surest ways to aggravate a slice is to try to keep the ball away from the rough on the right by pulling the arms to the left of the line of play. Try to push the ball out towards the right-hand edge of the fairway. It will be easier to do this if the left foot is advanced or the right foot drawn back a little at the address, for this position will help to counteract the tendency to pull in the arms. In this position you are more likely to hit the ball from inside-out.

Don't forget, however, to follow well through, otherwise the ball will be pushed out to the right, not sliced.   Play the ball at a point opposite the left heel ; and in addressing the ball tilt the head slightly to the right so that you will appear to be looking at the ball with the left eye.   This will help you to " hit past the chin ", as the Americans say.

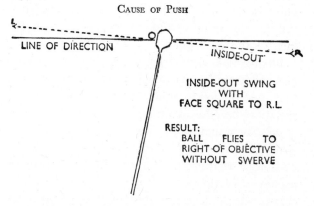

CAUSE OF PUSH

LINE OF DIRECTION

INSIDE-OUT

INSIDE-OUT SWING
WITH
FACE SQUARE TO R.L.

RESULT:
BALL   FLIES   TO
RIGHT OF OBJECTIVE
WITHOUT   SWERVE

Jones suggests a cure for slicing which, in some cases, may be effective but which we consider dangerous for beginners.   He advocates that the habitual slicer should grip the club with the right hand a bit more underneath the shaft, and that the face of the club should be open at the address. Then, Jones continues, he should swing well round his body and try to roll his wrists into the shot so that the club-face will be straight when it meets the ball.   This may be quite effective, but the success of the shot depends chiefly on the rolling of the wrists, which we regard as definitely dangerous and difficult. If the rolling of the wrists is not timed to a fraction of a second, the shot is just as likely to result in a slice or a hook.

Other causes of slicing may be mentioned, such as, failing to pivot sufficiently, too much right hand, and failing to follow through. But the chief cause is cutting across the ball through pulling the arms in towards the body with the face of the club open.

Slicing is a vicious habit and can lead to no end of trouble, particularly in a cross wind blowing from left to right. Under such conditions the slicer becomes more or less terrified before he plays ; he visualizes his shot sailing away with the wind far to the right of his objective. Again we emphasize that it is fatal to pull in the arms in an attempt to hold the ball up into the wind. Yet this is the fault committed by the majority of golfers. By all means allow for the wind, but instead of pulling in the arms, push them out, and follow through ; and, to assist you to do this, adopt a closed stance. If you connect properly, the ball should hold up into the wind. In any case, it has much more chance of finishing on the fairway.

If you are given to slicing you should examine the position of your hands on the grip at the address. You will probably find that you can see only one knuckle of your left hand. If so, you will reach the top of the swing with a very " open " face, and the face will still be open at impact. Turn the hands a little more over the shaft, that is, to the right, so that you can see three knuckles of the left hand.

It has been said that the majority of golfers fall into two classes—those who pull and those who slice, and that the " slicers " outnumber the " pullers " by five or six to one. The odds we believe to be even greater, but it suffices to say that the " slicers " far outnumber the " pullers ".

Hooking

A " hook " is the opposite of a " slice ". A slice fades to the right ; a hook veers to the left. It is a fault more peculiar to good golfers than to long-handicap players. Broadly speaking, this is due to the respective types of swings, the inside-out and the outside-in ; the former producing a hook, the latter a slice.

We have seen that a slice is generally caused by an outside-in swing with the face of the club open at impact, open to the direction followed by the club-head. A hook is caused correspondingly by an inside-out swing with the face of the club closed. A closed face is not in itself the cause of a hook ; it depends on the direction in which the club-head is travelling. If the club-head is travelling from inside-out, with the face closed, the result will be a hook, a hook of the worst type : the ball will fly out to the right then swing sharply to the left. If the club-head follows the line of direction, with a closed face, the ball will fly straight then veer to the left. But if the club-head travels from outside-in, with the face closed, the ball will fly straight to the left

CAUSE OF HOOK

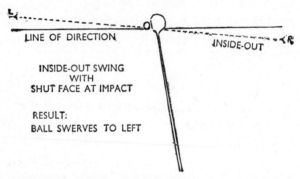

LINE OF DIRECTION

INSIDE-OUT

INSIDE-OUT SWING
WITH
SHUT FACE AT IMPACT

RESULT:
BALL SWERVES TO LEFT

with little or no hook, depending on how far the face is closed. This is a " pull " as distinct from a " hook ".

If one is addicted to hooking, the first thing to check is the position of the hands at the address. The " hooker " shows too many knuckles of the left hand, that is, it is turned too far over to the right ; and the right hand is generally too far under the shaft, that is, too far to the right. The Vs formed by the thumb and forefinger of each hand should point up the shaft, or no wider than the right shoulder, showing two or not more than three knuckles of the left hand, preferably two, if one is inclined to hook. With a " hooker's grip " the club-face is closed at the top of the swing ; the face is almost horizontal, looking upwards towards the heavens. With three knuckles showing, the face will be half shut ; with two

CAUSE OF PULL

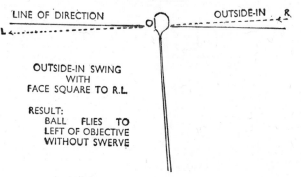

LINE OF DIRECTION   OUTSIDE-IN   R.

L

OUTSIDE-IN SWING
WITH
FACE SQUARE TO R.L.

RESULT:
    BALL   FLIES   TO
LEFT OF OBJECTIVE
WITHOUT SWERVE

knuckles showing, the face will be open, that is, almost vertical, with the toe of the club pointing downwards.

To-day, most of the leading players in America adopt a half-shut or shut position at the top of their swings. Vardon and Jones used an open face ; so does Cotton. It must be remembered that the American ball is larger than the British ball and tends to fly higher ; it also " sits up " more on the fairway than the smaller British ball.

FACE POINTING UPWARDS

HALF SHUT FACE
(FAVOURED BY MOST AMERICANS)

This partly accounts for the American method. And it must be remembered that Vardon learned to play with a gutta ball, which did not rise so easily as a rubber-cored ball. A shut face with a gutta ball would have produced little or no " carry ".

If the position of the hands is normal at the address, then watch how the hands start the back swing. Many players lift the club up steeply with the right hand instead of taking the club back all in one piece, with the left hand guiding and controlling the club. Lifting the club almost as soon as the back swing starts means that at the top of the swing the club-face will be shut ; and it is likely to remain so at impact.

Hooking can also be caused by excessive rolling of the wrists. At the start of the back swing, see whether the wrists roll to the right. If they do, there is every chance that they will roll too much to the left on the down swing. This fault is particularly common with those who have a very flat swing—a swing at the top of which the hands are below head level.

If you think you are not guilty of committing any of the aforementioned faults, it might be advisable to experiment along the following lines : (1) stand a little closer to the ball and slightly restrict the body turn ; or (2) adopt a slightly open stance ; or (3) play the ball a little further back.

Skying

If you look at a golfer's set of clubs you can sometimes get a fair idea of the owner's capabilities as a player. The wooden clubs of a novice, for instance, usually tell a tale. White paint marks can often be seen on the toe, heel, sole, and top of the club-heads. He has been hitting the ball with nearly every part of the head except the right part, the face.

When the white marks are seen on the top of the club it is obvious that skying has been the cause. Just as slicing is the opposite of hooking, skying is the opposite of topping. The ball soars in the air and travels only a short distance, considering the force that has been applied. Skying and topping can be traced to the same source. This may sound paradoxical but the fact remains. Once again the fault lies mainly in the early part of the back swing ; the club is lifted almost as soon as the back swing starts. Whether the ball is topped or skied depends where the club-head meets the ball on the sharp down swing, caused by the abrupt back swing. When the club-head hits the ground and ball simultaneously with this " chopping " down swing, a skied shot results. The ball is hit not with the face but above it, with the top of the club-head ; at impact the face is too far under the ball, just as it is too much above the ball in a topped shot. With wooden clubs, particularly the driver, the club-head should travel several inches parallel and close to the ground before making contact with the ball.

Rolling of the wrists can also cause skying. If there is a roll of the wrists on the back swing there may be an excessive roll from right to left on the down swing. If so, the club-head will be turned over and down. The ball may be skied or smothered, depending whether the ball is hit below or above middle.

What we have said about skying is applicable to wooden clubs only. Iron shots are skied by hitting the lower part of the ball with the face of the club open.

Sclaffing

Sclaffing is hitting the ground a few inches behind the ball. This, as we have seen, is also one of the main causes of topping ; the difference lies in where the club-face makes contact with the ball, just as it marks, as we have also noted, the difference between a topped and a skied shot. Thus topping, skying, and sclaffing are very closely related, more so than we would at first imagine.

In a sclaffed shot, the ball is hit just that little bit lower that prevents it from becoming a topped shot. The ball flies low for a short distance then rolls a comparatively long way, owing to the top

or over-spin imparted when the ball is hit just
above middle. One obvious reason for sclaffing
is the dropping of the right shoulder on the down
swing. But the real source of trouble begins
earlier. At the address the right shoulder may
be too far down. A more likely cause is bad
pivoting with a wrong distribution of the weight.
If, in the pivot, the left knee dips, with consequently too much weight on the left foot, the left

SCLAFFING—HITTING GROUND BEHIND BALL

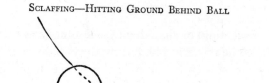

shoulder and head will also dip. The right
shoulder correspondingly will be that much
higher than the left at the top of the swing. This
position, coupled with too much weight on the
left foot, is simply inviting a sclaff. In addition,
from such a position, there is a very strong
tendency to " throw " the club-head out and
away from the body ; indeed, any other action
would be well-nigh impossible. It is for these
reasons that the right shoulder drops in the down
swing, causing the club-head to make contact
with the ground a few inches behind the ball.

E

If a sclaff does not result, then the ball will be topped, depending where the club-head makes contact with the ball.

It is necessary, then, to check the position of the shoulders at the address. Watch the pivot to see that the left knee is not dipped with too much weight on the left foot. And do not drop the right shoulder on the down swing.

Socketing

Socketing, or shanking as it is sometimes called, is, as the terms imply, hitting the ball not with the face of the club but with the socket or shank—that part of the head of an iron into which the shaft is inserted. The ball, as a result, flies off low and very sharply to the right. There is not a golfer worthy of the name but has at some time suffered from this affliction. To say the least, it is a most demoralizing experience.

So many theories have been advanced about the cause and cure of socketing that it is with some diffidence that we approach the subject. Socketing usually occurs when we play an approach shot, generally a comparatively short pitch with, say, the No. 7 iron. The cause, we believe, is a bent left arm at impact. It cannot be denied that, if the left arm is bent at impact, the socket and not the face of the club will present itself first to the ball. See then that the left arm is straight at impact. This is so important that it cannot be over-emphasized.

The bent left arm may be caused by a too vigorous use of the right arm, thus overpowering the left and causing it to bend by forcing the left elbow outwards. This can happen when a too determined effort is made to produce side-spin. The club-face is drawn across the ball with an exaggerated outside-in swing. Keep the left arm close to the body throughout the entire swing.

The wrong use of the wrists may also cause socketing. Do not " break " the wrists too soon on the back swing. The break should occur when the hands are almost waist high. In the same way the wrists should not be uncocked too soon on the down swing.

Socketing may be caused by moving the head at impact. This is due largely to over anxiety to see the result of the stroke. Keep the head down and steady is sound advice when playing a short pitch.

" Wait for it " is also a good maxim at any time. Some players are inclined to hit the ball too soon. The swing is so hurried throughout that the club-head does not get time to reach its proper position. If the club-head is not in the right position at the top of the swing it is not likely to reach the ball in the correct position at impact. A shanked shot may result.

Another possible cause of socketing has been

suggested to the writer by a beginner. We readily give it here, as we have never seen it stated ; and there is, we believe, at least a modicum of justification in what he affirms. Socketing, he asserts, is due to the player imagining that he is hitting the ball not with a club-head but with a stick, the stick being the shaft. He consequently hits the ball, so to speak, with the end of the shaft or socket. It should be realized that the purpose of the shaft is to impart speed to the club-head ; it is in no way a striking force.

As there are so many alleged cures for socketing, it is probably wiser to go back to first principles. The first thing to do is to get the right mental attitude. First, forget that such a thing as socketing ever existed. Then, to regain confidence, begin by playing very short chip shots from just off the green with a No. 7 iron. When you are satisfied that you are hitting these correctly, gradually increase the distance as your efforts meet with success. Should you still socket, we advise you to check up on your grip and the fundamental principles of the swing as stated in the chapter on " Approach Shots ", with particular reference to the No. 7 iron.

Rules of the Game of Golf
1st January, 1964

SECTION I

ETIQUETTE

1. No one should move, talk or stand close to or directly behind the ball or the hole when a player is addressing the ball or making a stroke.

2. The player who has the honour should be allowed to play before his opponent or fellow-competitor tees his ball.

3. No player should play until the players in front are out of range.

4. In the interest of all, players should play without delay.

5. Players searching for a ball should allow other players coming up to pass them; they should signal to the players following them to pass, and should not continue their play until those players have passed and are out of range.

6. Before leaving a bunker, a player should carefully fill up all holes made by him therein.

7. Through the green a player should ensure that any turf cut or displaced by him is replaced at once and pressed down, and that, after the players have holed out, any damage to the putting green made by the ball or the player is carefully repaired.

8. Players should ensure that, when dropping bags or the flagstick, no damage is done to the putting green, and that neither they nor their caddies damage the hole by standing close to the hole or in handling the flagstick. The flagstick should be properly replaced in the hole before the players leave the putting green.

9. When the play of a hole has been completed, players should immediately leave the putting green.

Priority on the course

In the absence of special rules, singles, threesomes or four-somes should have precedence of and be entitled to pass any other kind of match.   A single player has no standing, and should give way to a match of any kind.

Any match playing a whole round is entitled to pass a match playing a shorter round.

If a match fail to keep its place on the course and lose more than one clear hole on the players in front, it should allow the match following to pass.

SECTION II

DEFINITIONS

1. Addressing the ball

A player has " addressed the ball " when he has taken his stance by placing his feet on the ground in position for and preparatory to making a stroke and has also grounded his club, except that in a hazard a player has " addressed the ball " when he has taken his stance preparatory to making a stroke.

2. Advice

" Advice " is any counsel or suggestion which could influence a player in determining his play, the choice of a club, or the method of making a stroke.

Information on the Rules or Local Rules is not " advice."

3. Ball deemed to move

A ball is deemed to have " moved " if it leave its position and come to rest in any other place.

4. Ball holed

A ball is " holed " when it lies within the circumference of the hole and all of it is below the level of the lip of the hole.

5. Ball in play

A ball is " in play " as soon as the player has made a stroke on the teeing ground.   It remains in play as his ball until holed out, except when it is out of bounds, lost, or lifted, or another ball is substituted in accordance with the Rules or Local Rules.

6. Ball lost

A ball is " lost " if :

a. It be not found, or be not identified as his by the player, within five minutes after the player's side or his or their caddies have begun to search for it ; or

b. The player has put another ball into play under the Rules.

Play of another ball provisionally, or of a wrong ball, does not constitute abandonment of the ball in play. Time spent in playing a wrong ball is not counted in the five-minute period allowed for search.

7. Caddie, forecaddie and equipment

A " caddie " is one who carries or handles a player's clubs during play and otherwise assists him in accordance with the Rules.

A " forecaddie " is one employed by the Committee to indicate to players the position of balls on the course, and is an outside agency (Definition 22).

" Equipment " is anything used, worn or carried by or for the player except his ball in play.

8. Casual water

" Casual water " is any temporary accumulation of water which is visible before or after the player takes his stance and which is not a hazard of itself or is not in a water hazard. Snow and ice are " casual water " unless otherwise determined by Local Rule.

9. Committee

The " Committee " is the committee in charge of the competition.

10. Competitor

A " competitor " is a player in a stroke competition. A " fellow-competitor " is any player with whom the competitor plays. Neither is partner of the other.

In stroke play foursome and four-ball competitions, where the context so admits, the word " competitor " or " fellow-competitor " shall be held to include his partner.

11. Course

The " course " is the whole area within which play is permitted. It is the duty of the authorities in charge of the course to define its boundaries accurately.

12. Flagstick

The " flagstick " is a movable straight indicator provided by the Committee, with or without bunting or other material attached, centred in the hole to show its position. It shall be circular in cross-section.

13. Ground under repair

" Ground under repair " is any portion of the course so marked by order of the committee concerned or so declared by its authorized representative. It includes material piled for removal and a hole made by a greenkeeper, even if not so marked. Stakes and lines defining " ground under repair " are not in such ground.

14. Hazards

A " hazard " is any bunker or water hazard. Bare patches, scrapes, roads, tracks and paths are not " hazards."

a. A " bunker " is an area of bare ground, often a depression, which is usually covered with sand. Grass-covered ground bordering or within a " bunker " is *not* part of the " hazard."

b. A " water hazard " is any sea, lake, pond, river, ditch, surface drainage ditch or other open water course (regardless of whether or not it contains water), and anything of a similar nature.

All ground or water within the margin of a water hazard, whether or not it be covered with any growing substance, is part of the water hazard.

c. A " lateral water hazard " is a water hazard or that part of a water hazard running approximately parallel to the line of play and so situated that it is not possible or is deemed by the Committee to be impracticable to drop a ball behind the water hazard and keep the spot at which the ball last crossed the hazard margin between the player and the hole.

d. It is the duty of the Committee in charge of a course to define accurately the extent of the hazards and water hazards when there is any doubt. That part of a hazard to be played as a lateral water hazard should be distinctively marked. Stakes and lines defining the boundaries of hazards are not in the hazards.

15. Hole

The " hole " shall be $4\frac{1}{4}$ inches in diameter and at least 4 inches deep. If a lining be used, it shall be sunk at least 1 inch below the putting green surface unless the nature of the soil makes it impractical to do so ; its outer diameter shall not exceed $4\frac{1}{4}$ inches.

16. Honour

The side which is entitled to play first from the teeing ground is said to have the " honour."

17. Loose impediments

The term " loose impediments " denotes natural objects not fixed or growing and not adhering to the ball, and includes stones not solidly embedded, leaves, twigs, branches and the like, dung, worms and insects and casts or heaps made by them.

18. Marker

A " maker " is a scorer in stroke play who is appointed by the Committee to record a competitor's score. He may be a fellow-competitor. He is not a referee.

A marker should not lift the ball or mark its position and, unless he is a fellow-competitor, should not attend the flagstick or stand at the hole or mark its position.

19. Observer

An " observer " is appointed by the Committee to assist a referee to decide questions of fact and to report to him any breach of a Rule or Local Rule. An observer should not attend the flagstick, stand at or mark the position of the hole, or lift the ball or mark its position.

20. Obstructions

An " obstruction " is anything artificial, whether erected, placed or left on the course, except:

    a. Objects defining out of bounds, such as walls, fences, stakes, and railings;

    b. Artificial surfaces and sides of roads and paths;

    c. In water hazards, artificially surfaced banks or beds, including bridge supports when part of such a bank. Bridges and bridge supports which are not part of such a bank are obstructions;

    d. Any construction declared by the Committee to be an integral part of the course.

21. Out of bounds

" Out of bounds " is ground on which play is prohibited.

When out of bounds is fixed by stakes or a fence, the out of bounds line is determined by the nearest inside points of the stakes or fence posts at ground level; the line extends upwards. When out of bounds is fixed by a line on the ground, the line itself is out of bounds.

A ball is out of bounds when all of it lies out of bounds.

22. Outside agency

An " outside agency " is any agency not part of the match or, in stroke play, not part of a competitor's side, and includes a referee, a marker, an observer, or a forecaddie employed by the Committee.

23. Partner

A " partner " is a player associated with another player on the same side.

In a threesome, foursome or a four-ball where the context so admits, the word " player " shall be held to include his partner.

24. Penalty stroke

A " penalty stroke " is one added to the score of a side under certain Rules. It does not affect the order of play.

25. Putting green

The " putting green " is all ground of the hole being played which is specially prepared for putting or otherwise defined as such by the Committee.

26. Referee

A " referee " is a person who has been appointed by the Committee to accompany players to decide questions of fact and of golf law. He shall act on any breach of Rule or Local Rule which he may observe or which may be reported to him by an observer (Definition 19).

In stroke play the Committee may limit a referee's duties.

A referee should not attend the flagstick, stand at or mark the position of the hole, or lift the ball or mark its position.

27. Rub of the green

A " rub of the green " occurs when a ball in motion is stopped or deflected by any outside agency.

28. Sides and matches

Side : A player, or two or more players who are partners.

Single : A match in which one plays against another.

Threesome : A match in which one plays against two, and each side plays one ball.

Foursome : A match in which two play against two, and each side plays one ball.

Three-Ball : A match in which three play against one another, each playing his own ball.

Best-Ball : A match in which one plays against the better ball of two or the best ball of three players.

Four-Ball : A match in which two play their better ball against the better ball of two other players.

Note: In a best-ball or four-ball match, if a partner be absent for reasons satisfactory to the Committee, the remaining member(s) of his side may represent the side.

29. Stipulated round

The " stipulated round " consists of playing the eighteen holes of the course in their correct sequence, unless otherwise authorized by the Committee.

30. Stroke

A " stroke " is the forward movement of the club made with the intention of fairly striking at and moving the ball.

31. Teeing

In " teeing," the ball may be placed on the ground or on sand or other substance in order to raise it off the ground.

32. Teeing ground

The " teeing ground " is the starting place for the hole to be played. It is a rectangular area two club-lengths in depth, the front and the sides of which are defined by the outside limits of two markers. A ball is outside the teeing ground when all of it lies outside the stipulated area.

33. Terms used in reckoning

The reckoning of holes is kept by the terms :—so many " holes up " or " all square ", and so many " to play ".

A side is " dormie " when it is as many holes up as there are holes remaining to be played.

34. Through the green

" Through the green " is the whole area of the course except :—
  a. Teeing ground and putting green of the hole being played ;
  b. All hazards on the course.

SECTION III
THE RULES OF PLAY
RULE 1. THE GAME

The Game of Golf consists in playing a ball from the teeing ground into the hole by successive strokes in accordance with the Rules.

Penalty for breach of Rule :
Match play—Loss of hole; Stroke play—Disqualification

RULE 2. THE CLUB AND THE BALL

The Royal and Ancient Golf Club of St. Andrews, Scotland, and the United States Golf Association, reserve the right to change the Rules and the interpretations regulating clubs and balls at any time.

1. Legal clubs and balls

Players shall use clubs and balls which conform with Clauses 2 and 3 of this Rule.

2. Form and make of clubs
a. General characteristics

The golf club shall be composed of a shaft and a head, and all of the various parts shall be fixed so that the club is one unit.

The club shall not be substantially different from the traditional and customary form and make.

An " iron " club is one with a head which usually is relatively narrow from face to back, and usually is made of steel.

A " wood " club is one with a head relatively broad from face to back, and usually made of wood, plastic or a light metal.

" A putter " is a club designed primarily for use on the putting green—see Definition 25.

b. **Movable parts prohibited**

No part of the club may be movable or separable or capable of adjustment during a round of play.

The player or other agency shall not change the playing characteristics of a club during a round.

c. **Shape of head**

The length of a club head shall be greater than the breadth. Length shall be determined on a horizontal line, five-eighths of an inch above the sole, from the back of the heel to the end of the toe or a vertical projection thereof.

Breadth shall be determined on a horizontal line between the outermost points of the face and the back of the head or vertical projections thereof.

d. **Face of head**

Club faces shall not embody any degree of concavity on the hitting surface and shall not bear any lines, dots or other markings with sharp or rough edges, or any type of finish made for the purpose of putting additional spin on the ball.

The club shall have only one face designed for striking the ball. However, a putter may have two faces if the loft of both faces is practically the same.

Iron clubs.—The face of an iron club shall not contain an inset or attachment.

Markings on the face of an iron club shall conform with Royal and Ancient specifications (see Note to this Rule).

e. **Shaft**

The shaft shall be fixed to the club head at the heel, either directly or by attachment to a neck or socket.

The shaft and the neck or socket shall remain in line with the heel, or with a point to right or left of the heel, when the club is soled at address. The distance between the axis of the shaft (or the neck or socket) and the back of the heel shall not exceed five-eighths of an inch in wood clubs and five-sixteenths in iron clubs.

Exception for putters.—The shaft of a putter may be fixed at any point in the head and need not remain in line with the heel. (A putter is a club designed primarily for use on the putting green—see Definition 25.)

f. Grip

The grip shall be a continuation of the shaft to which material may be added for the purpose of obtaining a firm hold. The grip shall be substantially straight and plain in form, may have flat sides, but shall not have a channel or a furrow or be moulded for any part of the hands.

A device designed to give the player artificial aid in gripping or swinging the club shall be deemed to violate this Rule even though it be not a part of the club.

(Other artificial devices—Rule 37-9.)

NOTE: Players in doubt as to the legality of clubs are advised to consult the Royal and Ancient Golf Club. Specifications for markings on iron clubs have been issued to manufacturers.

If a manufacturer is in doubt as to the legality of a club which he proposes to manufacture, he should submit a sample to the Royal and Ancient Golf Club for a ruling, such sample to become the property of the Royal and Ancient Golf Club for reference purposes.

3. Weight and size of ball

The weight of the ball shall be *not greater* than 1·620 ounces avoirdupois, and the size *not less* than 1·620 inches in diameter.

Penalty for breach of rule: Disqualification

NOTE: In the U.S.A. the weight of the ball shall be not greater than 1·620 ounces avoirdupois and the size not less than 1·680 inches in diameter, but in international team competitions the size of the ball shall be not less than 1·620 inches in diameter.

RULE 3. MAXIMUM OF FOURTEEN CLUBS

1. Selection and replacement of clubs

Before starting a stipulated round a player shall select his clubs, which must not exceed fourteen in number. He is limited to the clubs so selected for that round except that, without unduly delaying play, he may:—

    a. If he started with fewer than fourteen, add as many as will bring his total to that number ;

    b. Replace a club which becomes unfit for play in the normal course of play.

The addition or replacement of a club or clubs may not be made by borrowing from any other person playing on the course.

Penalty for breach of Rule 3-1:

* Match play—loss of one hole for each excess club at each hole at which violation occurred ; maximum penalty per round: loss of two holes for each excess club. The penalty shall be applied on discovery of the violation and without changing the number of holes remaining to be played.

Stroke play—Two strokes for each excess club at each hole at which violation occurred ; maximum penalty per round: four strokes for each excess club.

* The penalty applies during the round or, in the discretion of the Committee, after the round even though a claim has not been made within the time limit stipulated in Rule 11-1.

SECTION IV

THE RULES OF PLAY

RULE 4. AGREEMENT TO WAIVE RULES PROHIBITED

Players shall not agree to exclude the operation of any Rule or Local Rule or to waive any penalty incurred.

Penalty for breach of Rule:
Match play—Disqualification of both sides ;
Stroke play—Disqualification of competitors concerned

RULE 5. GENERAL PENALTY

Except when otherwise provided for, the penalty for a breach of a Rule or Local Rule is :

Match play—Loss of hole ;
Stroke play—Two strokes

RULE 6. MATCH PLAY

1. Winner of hole

In match play the game is played by holes.

Except as otherwise provided for in the Rules, a hole is won by the side which holes its ball in the fewer strokes. In a handicap match the lower net score wins the hole.

2. Halved hole

A hole is halved if each side holes out in the same number of strokes.

When a player has holed out and his opponent has been left with a stroke for the half, nothing that the player who has holed out can do shall deprive him of the half which he has already gained ; but if the player thereafter incur any penalty, he shall concede the half of the hole to his opponent.

3. Winner of match

A match (which consists of a stipulated round, unless otherwise decreed by the Committee) is won by the side which is leading by a number of holes greater than the number of holes remaining to be played.

RULE 7. STROKE PLAY

1. General rule

The Rules for match play, so far as they are not at variance with specific Rules for stroke play, shall apply to stroke competitions. The converse is not true.

2. Winner

The competitor who holes the stipulated round or rounds in the fewest strokes is the winner.

RULE 8. PRACTICE

1. During play of hole

During the play of a hole, a player shall not play any practice stroke.

Penalty for breach of Rule 8-1 :
Match play—Loss of hole ; Stroke play—Two strokes

2. Between holes

Between the play of two holes, a player shall not play any practice stroke from any hazard, or on or to the putting green other than that of the hole last played.

Penalty for breach of Rule 8-2 :
*Match play—Loss of hole ; Stroke play—Two strokes
*The penalty applies to the next hole

3. Stroke play: before round

On any day of a stroke competition or play-off, a competitor shall not practise on the competition course before a round or play-off. When a competition extends over consecutive days, practise on the competition course between rounds is prohibited.

NOTE: The Committee may at its discretion waive, or modify these prohibitions in the conditions of the competition (Appendix 1-3).

Penalty for breach of Rule 8-3:
Disqualification
(*Duty of Committee to define practice ground—Rule 36-4b.*)

NOTE 1. A practice swing is not a practice stroke and may be taken at any place on the course provided the player does not violate the Rules.
NOTE 2. Unless otherwise decided by the Committee, there is no penalty for practice on the course on any day of a match play competition.

RULE 9. ADVICE (DEF. 2)

1. Giving or asking for advice

A player or a competitor shall not give or ask for advice or take any action which may result in his receiving advice except from his caddie, his partner, or his partner's caddie.

2. Indicating line of play

Except on the putting green, a player may have the line of play indicated to him by anyone, but no mark shall be placed on the line, nor shall anyone stand on or close to the line while the stroke is being played.

(Indicating line of play on putting green—Rule 35-1e)

Penalty for breach of Rule:

Match play—Loss of hole; Stroke play—Two strokes

RULE 10: INFORMATION AS TO STROKES TAKEN

1. General

A player who has incurred a penalty shall state the fact to his opponent or marker as soon as possible. The number of strokes a player has taken shall include any penalty strokes incurred.

2. Match play

A player is entitled at any time during the play of a hole to ascertain from his opponent the number of strokes the latter has taken. If the opponent give wrong information as to the number of strokes he has taken and correct his mistake before the player has played his next stroke, he shall incur no penalty ; if he fail to do so, *he shall lose the hole.*

RULE 11. DISPUTES, DECISIONS AND DOUBT AS TO RIGHTS

1. Claims and Penalties

a. Match play

In match play, if a dispute or doubt arise between the players on any point, in order that a claim may be considered it must be made before any player in the match plays from the next teeing ground, or, in the case of the last hole of the round, before all players in the match leave the putting green. Any later claim based on newly discovered facts cannot be considered unless the player making the claim had been given wrong information by an opponent.

(*Maximum of fourteen clubs—Rule 3*)

b. **Stroke play**

In stroke play no penalty shall be imposed after the competition is closed unless wrong information had been given by the competitor. A competition is deemed to have closed :

In stroke play only—When the result of the competition is officially announced ;

In stroke play qualifying followed by match play—When the player has teed off in his first match.

2. **Referee's decision**

If a referee has been appointed by the Committee his decision shall be final.

3. **Committee's decision**

In the absence of a referee, the players shall refer any dispute to the Committee, whose decision shall be final.

If the Committee cannot come to a decision, it shall refer the dispute to the Rules of Golf Committee of the Royal and Ancient Golf Club of St. Andrews, whose decision shall be final.

If the point in dispute or doubt has not been referred to the Rules of Golf Committee the player or players have the right to refer an agreed statement through the Secretary of the Club to the Rules of Golf Committee for an opinion as to the correctness of the decision given. The reply will be sent to the Secretary of the Club or Clubs concerned.

If play be conducted other than in accordance with the Rules of Golf, the Rules of Golf Committee will not give a decision on any question.

4. **Decision by equity**

If any point in dispute be not covered by the Rules or Local Rules, the decision shall be made in accordance with equity.

5. **Stroke play : doubt as to procedure**

In stroke play only, when a competitor is doubtful of his rights or procedure, he may play out the hole with the ball in play and, at the same time, complete the play of the hole with a second ball. Before playing a stroke with either ball, the competitor must announce to his marker his intention to proceed under this Rule and must announce which ball he wants to score with if the Rules permit.

On completing the round, the competitor must report the facts immediately to the Committee. If it be found that the Rules allow the procedure selected in advance by the competitor, the score with the ball so selected shall be his score for the hole. Should the competitor fail to announce in advance his procedure or selection, the score with the second ball shall be his score for the hole if played in accordance with the Rules.

NOTE 1: The sole purpose of this Rule is to enable a competitor to avoid disqualification when doubtful of his rights or procedure; a competitor is not permitted to play in two ways and then choose his score.

NOTE 2: The privilege of playing a second ball does not exist in match play. A second ball played under Rule 11-5 is not a provisional ball under Rule 30.

SECTION V

THE RULES OF PLAY

RULE 12. THE HONOUR (DEF. 16)

1. The honour

a. Match play

A match begins by each side playing a ball from the first teeing ground in the order of the draw. In the absence of a draw, the option of taking the honour shall be decided by lot.

The side which wins a hole shall take the honour at the next teeing ground. If a hole has been halved, the side which had the honour at the previous teeing ground shall retain it.

b. Stroke play

The honour shall be taken as in match play.

2. Second ball from tee

If a player has to play a second ball from the tee, he shall do so after the opponent or fellow-competitor has played his first stroke.

3. Playing out of turn

a. Match play

If, on the teeing ground, a player play when his opponent should have played, the opponent may immediately require the player to abandon the ball so played and to play a ball in correct order, without penalty.

b. Stroke play

If, on the teeing ground, a competitor by mistake play out of turn, no penalty shall be incurred and the ball shall be played.

RULE 13. PLAYING OUTSIDE TEEING GROUND
(DEF. 32)

1. Match play

If a player, when starting a hole, play a ball from outside the teeing ground, the opponent may immediately require the player to replay the stroke, in which case the player shall tee a ball and play the stroke from within the teeing ground, without penalty.

2. Stroke play

If a competitor, when starting a hole, play his first stroke from outside the teeing ground, he shall count that stroke and any subsequent stroke so played and then play from within the teeing ground with the privilege of teeing his ball.

Penalty for breach of Rule 13-2: Disqualification

NOTE: **Stance**—*A player may take his stance outside the teeing ground to play a ball within it.*

RULE 14. BALL FALLING OFF TEE

If a ball, when not in play, fall off a tee or be knocked off a tee by the player in addressing it, it may be re-teed without penalty, but if a stroke be made at the ball in these circumstances, whether the ball be moving or not, the stroke shall be counted but no penalty shall be incurred.

RULE 15. ORDER OF PLAY IN THREESOME OR FOURSOME

1. General

In a threesome or a foursome, the partners shall strike off alternately from the teeing grounds, and thereafter shall strike alternately during the play of each hole. Penalty strokes (Definition 24) do not affect the order of play.

2. Match play

If a player play when his partner should have played, *his side shall lose the hole.*

3. Stroke play

If the partners play a stroke or strokes in incorrect order, such stroke or strokes shall be cancelled, and *the side shall be penalized two strokes.* A ball shall then be put in play as nearly as possible at the spot from which the side first played in incorrect order. This must be done before a stroke has been played from the next teeing ground, or, in the case of the last hole of the round, before the side has left the putting green. If they fail to do so, *they shall be disqualified.* If the first ball was played from the teeing ground, a ball may be teed anywhere within the teeing ground ; if from through the green or a hazard, it shall be dropped ; if on the putting green, it shall be placed.

SECTION VI

THE RULES OF PLAY

RULE 16. BALL PLAYED AS IT LIES AND NOT TOUCHED

The ball shall be played as it lies and shall not be purposely moved or purposely touched except that the player may, without penalty, touch his ball with his club in the act of addressing it and except as otherwise provided in the Rules or Local Rules.

Penalty for breach of Rule:

Match play—Loss of hole; Stroke play—Two strokes

(Ball moved accidentally by player—Rule 27-1c)

(Ball moved accidentally after address—Rule 27-1d)

RULE 17. IMPROVING LIE OR STANCE PROHIBITED

1. Improving line of play or lie prohibited

A player shall not improve, or allow to be improved, his line of play or the position or lie of his ball by moving, bending or breaking anything fixed or growing, or by removing or pressing down sand, loose soil, cut turf placed in position or other irregularities of surface which could in any way affect a player's lie, except :—

a. As may occur in the course of fairly taking his stance ;

b. In making the stroke or the backward movement of his club for the stroke ;

c. When teeing a ball ;

d. In repairing damage to the putting green under Rule 31-1.

The club may be grounded only lightly and must not be pressed on the ground.

(Removal of obstructions—Rule 31-1.)

NOTE: Things fixed include objects defining out of bounds.

2. Long grass and bushes

If a ball lie in long grass, rushes, bushes, whins, heather or the like, only so much thereof shall be touched as will enable the player to find and identify his ball ; nothing shall be done which may in any way improve its lie.

The player is not of necessity entitled to see the ball when playing a stroke.

3. Building of stance prohibited

A player is always entitled to place his feet firmly on the ground when taking his stance, but he is not allowed to build a stance.

4. Exerting influence on ball

No player or caddie shall take any action to influence the position or the movement of a ball except in accordance with the Rules.

Penalty for breach of Rule:

Match play—Loss of hole; Stroke play—Two strokes

NOTE: In the case of a serious breach of Rule 17-4, the Committee may impose a penalty of disqualification.

RULE 18. LOOSE IMPEDIMENTS (DEF. 17)

1. Removal of impediments

Any loose impediments may be removed without penalty except when both the impediment and the ball lie in or touch a hazard. When a ball is in motion, a loose impediment shall not be removed.

Penalty for breach of Rule 18-1:

Match play—Loss of hole; Stroke play—Two strokes

(Finding ball in hazard—Rule 33-1e)

2. Ball moved

Through the green, if the ball move after any loose impediment lying within a club-length of it has been touched by the player, his partner or either of their caddies, the player shall be deemed to have caused the ball to move. *The penalty shall be one stroke,* and the ball shall be played as it lies.

(Loose impediments on putting green—Rule 35-1b.)

RULE 19. STRIKING AT BALL

1. Ball to be fairly struck at

The ball shall be fairly struck at with the head of the club and must not be pushed, scraped or spooned.

Penalty for breach of Rule 19-1:

Match play—Loss of hole; Stroke play—Two strokes

2. Striking ball twice

If the player strike the ball twice when making a stroke, he shall count the stroke and *add a penalty stroke*, making two strokes in all.

(Playing a moving ball—Rule 25.)

RULE 20.   BALL FARTHER FROM THE HOLE PLAYED FIRST

1. General

When the balls are in play, the ball farther from the hole shall be played first. If the balls are equi-distant from the hole, the option of playing first shall be decided by lot.

A player or a competitor incurs no penalty if a ball is moved in measuring to determine which ball is farther from the hole. A ball so moved shall be replaced.

2. Match play

Through the green or in a hazard, if a player play when his opponent should have done so, the opponent may immediately require the player to replay the stroke. In such a case, the player shall drop a ball as near as possible to the spot from which his previous stroke was played, and play in correct order without penalty.

Penalty for breach of Rule 20-2:
Loss of hole

(Playing out of turn on putting green—Rule 35-2b.)

3. Stroke play

If a competitor play out of turn, no penalty shall be incurred. The ball shall be played as it lies.

SECTION VII

THE RULES OF PLAY

RULE 21.   PLAYING A WRONG BALL OR UNDER A WRONG RULE

1. General: Holing out original ball

A player must hole out with the ball driven from the teeing ground unless a Rule or Local Rule permits him to substitute another ball.

2. Match play

a. Wrong ball

If a player play a stroke with a ball other than his own except in a hazard, *he shall lose the hole.* There is no penalty if a player play a stroke or strokes in a hazard with a ball other than his own, provided he then play his own ball ; the strokes so played with a ball other than the player's own do not count in the player's score.

When the player and the opponent exchange balls, the first to play the wrong ball shall lose the hole; when this cannot be determined, the hole shall be played out with the balls exchanged.

b. **Ball played under wrong Rule**

If a player play a stroke under a Rule which does not govern the particular case, *he shall lose the hole.*

3. Stroke play

a. **Wrong ball**

If a competitor play a stroke or strokes with a ball other than his own, except in a hazard, he shall *add two penalty strokes* to his score for the hole and shall then play his own ball. Strokes played by a competitor with a ball other than his own do not count in his score. There is no penalty for a competitor playing a stroke or strokes with a wrong ball in a hazard provided he then play his own ball.

b. **Ball played under wrong Rule**

If a competitor play a stroke or strokes under a Rule which does not govern the particular case, he shall *add two penalty strokes* to his score for the hole and shall then proceed under a Rule which governs the case. Strokes played by a competitor under a Rule which does not govern the particular case do not count in his score.

c. **Rectification after holing out**

If a competitor hole out with a ball other than his own or a ball played under a Rule not governing the particular case, he may rectify his mistake by proceeding in accordance with Rule 21-3, subject to the prescribed penalty, provided he has not made a stroke on the next teeing ground, or, in the case of the last hole of the round, has not left the putting green. *The competitor shall be disqualified* if he does not rectify his mistake.

RULE 22. LIFTING, DROPPING AND PLACING

1. Lifting

a. **By whom**

A ball to be lifted under the Rules or the Local Rules may be lifted by the owner, his partner or either of their caddies, or by another person authorized by the owner. In any case the owner shall be responsible for any breach of the Rules or Local Rules.

b. **Before holing out in stroke play**

If a competitor's ball be lifted before it is holed out, except as provided for in the Rules or Local Rules, the competitor shall replace it *under a penalty of two strokes*, provided he does as before he has played a stroke from the next teeing ground, or, in the case of the last hole of the round, before he has left the putting green. If he fail so to replace it, *he shall be disqualified.*

(Procedure in discontinuing play—Rule 37-6b.)

(Ball moved by outside agency—Rule 27-1a.)

2. Dropping

a. **How to drop**

A ball to be dropped under the Rules or Local Rules shall be dropped by the player himself. He shall face the hole, stand erect, and drop the ball behind him over his shoulder. If a ball be dropped in any other manner and remains the ball in play (Definition 5), *the player shall incur a penalty stroke.*

If the ball touch the player, or if it come to rest against the player and move when he then moves, there is no penalty, and the ball shall be played as it lies.

b. **Where to drop**

When a ball is to be dropped it shall be dropped as near as possible to the spot where the ball lay, except when a Rule permits it to be dropped elsewhere or placed. In a hazard, the ball must be dropped and come to rest in that hazard ; if it rolls out of the hazard, it must be re-dropped, without penalty.

c. **Rolling into hazard, out of bounds or two club-lengths**

If a dropped ball roll out of bounds or into a hazard it may be re-dropped, without penalty. If a dropped ball roll more than two club-lengths from the point where it first struck the ground, it shall be re-dropped, without penalty. If the configuration of the ground makes it impossible to prevent the ball from so rolling, it may be placed at the point where the ball was last dropped.

d. **Rolling nearer hole**

If a dropped ball come to rest nearer the hole than its original position, it shall be re-dropped, without penalty. If the configuration of the ground makes it impossible to prevent the ball from coming to rest nearer the hole, it shall be placed, without penalty.

Penalty for breach of Rule 22-2:
Match play—Loss of hole; Stroke play—Two strokes

3. Placing

a. How and where to place

A ball to be placed or replaced under the Rules or Local Rules shall be placed by the player, his partner, or either of their caddies on the spot where the ball lay, except when a Rule permits it to be placed elsewhere.

b. Lie of lifted ball altered

If the original lie of a ball to be placed or replaced has been altered in the play of another ball, the ball shall be placed as near as possible to, but not nearer the hole than, the spot where it lay and in a lie similar to that which it originally occupied.

c. Spot not determinable

If it be impossible to determine the spot where the ball is to be placed, through the green or in a hazard the ball shall be dropped, or on the putting green it shall be placed, as near as possible to the place where it lay, but not nearer the hole.

d. Ball moving

If a ball fail to come to rest on the spot on which it was being placed, it must be replaced, without penalty.

Penalty for breach of Rule 22-3:
Match play—Loss of hole; Stroke play—Two strokes

4. Ball in play when dropped or placed

A ball dropped or placed under a Rule governing the particular case is in play (Definition 5) and shall not be lifted or re-dropped or replaced except as provided in the Rules.

5. Lifting ball wrongly dropped or placed

A ball dropped or placed but not played may be lifted without penalty if:

a. It was dropped or placed under a Rule governing the particular case but not in the right place or otherwise not in accordance with that Rule (except a ball improperly dropped under Rule 22-1). The player shall then drop or place the ball in accordance with the governing Rule.

b. It was dropped or placed under a Rule which does not govern the particular case. The player shall then proceed under a Rule which governs the case. However, in match play, if, before the opponent plays his next stroke, the player fail to inform him that the ball has been lifted, *the player shall lose the hole.*

NOTE: In stroke play a serious breach of Rule 22 should be dealt with by the Committee under Rule 1.

RULE 23. IDENTIFYING OR CLEANING BALL

The responsibility for playing the proper ball rests with the player. Each player should put an identification mark on his ball.

1. Identifying ball

Except in a hazard the player may, without penalty, lift his ball in play for the purpose of identification, provided he replace it on the spot from which it was lifted, provided this is done in the presence of his opponent in match play or marker in stroke play.

(Touching grass, etc., for identification—Rule 17-2.)

2. Cleaning ball

A ball may be cleaned when lifted on the putting green under Rule 35-1d or when lifted from a water hazard, an unplayable lie, casual water, ground under repair or under Rule 32 ; otherwise, during the play of a hole a player may not clean a ball, except to the extent necessary for identification or if permitted by Local Rule.

Penalty for breach of Rule 23-1 or 2:
Match play—Loss of hole; Stroke play—Two strokes

RULE 24. BALL INTERFERING WITH PLAY

Through the green or in a hazard, a player may have any other ball lifted if he consider that it might interfere with his play. A ball so lifted shall be replaced after the player has played his stroke.

If a ball be accidentally moved in complying with this Rule, no penalty shall be incurred and the ball so moved shall be replaced.

(Lie of lifted ball altered—Rule 22-3b.)

(Putting green—Rule 35-2a and 3a.)

Penalty for breach of Rule:
Match play—Loss of hole; Stroke play—Two strokes

RULE 25. A MOVING BALL

1. Playing moving ball prohibited

A player shall not play while his ball is moving.
Exceptions:
Ball falling off tee—Rule 14.
Striking ball twice—Rule 19-2.
As hereunder—Rule 25-2.

When the ball only begins to move after the player has begun the stroke or the backward movement of his club for the stroke, he shall incur no penalty under this Rule, but he is not exempted from the provisions for :—

Ball moving after removal of loose impediment—Rules 18-2 and 27-1e.

Ball moved accidentally by player—Rule 27-1c.

Ball moving after it has been addressed—Rule 27-1d.

2. Ball moving in water

When a ball is in water, the player may, without penalty, make a stroke at it while it is moving, but he must not delay to make his stroke in order to allow the wind or current to better the position of the ball.

Penalty for breach of Rule:
Match play—Loss of hole; Stroke play—Two strokes

RULE 26. BALL IN MOTION STOPPED OR DEFLECTED

1. General

a. By outside agency

If a ball in motion be accidentally stopped or deflected by any outside agency, it is a rub of the green and the ball shall be played as it lies, without penalty.

b. Lodging in outside agency

If a ball lodge in anything moving, the player shall, through the green or in a hazard, drop a ball, or on the putting green place a ball, as near as possible to the spot where the object was when the ball lodged in it, without penalty.

2. Match play

a. By player

If a player's ball be stopped or deflected by himself, his partner or either of their caddies or equipment, *he shall lose the hole.*

b. By opponent

If a player's ball be stopped or deflected by an opponent, his caddie or equipment, *the opponent's side shall lose the hole.*

(Ball striking opponent's ball : Rule 27-2b.)

Exception: Ball striking person attending flagstick—Rule 34-4a.

3. Stroke play

a. By competitor

If a competitor's ball be stopped or deflected by himself, his partner or either of their caddies or equipment, *the competitor shall incur a penalty of two strokes.* The ball shall be played as it lies, except when it lodges in the competitor's, his partner's or either of their caddies' clothes or equipment, in which case the competitor shall, through the green or in a hazard, drop the ball, or on the putting green place the ball, as near as possible to where the article was when the ball lodged in it.

b. By fellow-competitor

If a competitor's ball be accidentally stopped or deflected by a fellow-competitor, his caddie, ball or equipment, it is a rub of the green and the ball shall be played as it lies.

Exceptions:

Ball lodging in fellow-competitor's clothes, etc.—Clause 1b of this Rule.

Ball striking fellow-competitor's ball on the putting green or within 20 yards of hole—Rule 35-3c.

Ball striking person attending flagstick—Rule 34-4a.

Penalty for breach of Rule:

Match play—Loss of hole; Stroke play—Two strokes

NOTE: If the referee or the Committee determine that a ball has been deliberately stopped or deflected by an outside agency, including a fellow-competitor or his caddie, further procedure should be prescribed in equity under Rule 11-4.

RULE 27. BALL AT REST MOVED (DEF. 3)

1. General

a. By outside agency

If a ball at rest be moved by any outside agency except wind, the owner shall incur no penalty and shall replace the ball before playing another stroke.

(Opponent's ball moved by player's ball—Rule 27-2b.)

NOTE: If the ball moved is not immediately recoverable, another ball may be substituted.

b. During search

During search for a ball, if it be moved by an opponent, a fellow-competitor or the caddie of either, no penalty shall be incurred. The player shall replace the ball before playing another stroke.

c. By player, accidentally

When a ball is in play, if a player, his partner, or either of their caddies accidentally move it, or by touching anything cause it to move (except as otherwise provided for in the

Rules), *the player shall incur a penalty stroke* and the ball shall be played as it lies.

(Ball purposely moved or purposely touched—Rule 16.)

d. Ball moving accidentally after address

If a ball in play move after the player has addressed it (Definition 1), he shall be deemed to have caused it to move and *shall incur a penalty stroke*, and the ball shall be played as it lies.

(Ball purposely moved or purposely touched—Rule 16.)

e. Touching loose impediment

If a player has touched a loose impediment (Rules 18 and 35-1b) and the ball move, but not until the player has addressed it (Definition 1), he shall be deemed to have caused it to move under paragraph d above, and *shall incur a penalty stroke*. The ball shall be played as it lies.

2. Match play

a. By opponent

If a player's ball be touched or moved by an opponent, his caddie or equipment (except as otherwise provided in the Rules), *the opponent shall incur a penalty stroke*. The player shall replace the ball before playing another stroke.

b. Opponent's ball moved by player's ball

If a player's ball move an opponent's ball, no penalty shall be incurred. The opponent may either play his ball as it lies or, before another stroke is played by either side, he may replace the ball.

If the player's ball stop on the spot formerly occupied by the opponent's ball and the opponent declare his intention to replace his ball, the player shall first play another stroke, after which the opponent shall replace his ball.

(Putting green—Rule 35-2c.)

(Three-Ball, Best-Ball and Four-Ball match play—Rule 40-1c.)

3. Stroke play

Ball moved by fellow-competitor

If a competitor's ball be moved by a fellow-competitor, his caddie, his ball or equipment, no penalty shall be incurred. The competitor shall replace his ball before playing another stroke.

Exception to penalty: Ball striking fellow-competitor's ball on putting green or within 20 yards of hole—Rule 35-3c.

Penalty for breach of Rule:
Match play—Loss of hole; *Stroke play—Two strokes

*NOTE: A serious breach of this Rule should be dealt with by the Committee under Rule 1.

RULE 28. BALL UNFIT FOR PLAY

If the ball becomes so damaged as to be unfit for play, the player may substitute another ball, placing it on the spot where the original ball lay. Substitution may only be made on the hole during the play of which the damage occurred and in the presence of the opponent in match play or the marker in stroke play.

Penalty for breach of Rule:

Match play—Loss of hole; Stroke play—Two strokes

(Ball unplayable—Rule 29-2)

NOTE 1: *Mud or loose impediments adhering to a ball do not make it unfit for play.*

NOTE 2: *Where the existence of mud could become an encumbrance to play, the Committee should frame a Local Rule providing for the removal of mud.*

RULE 29. BALL LOST (DEF. 6),
OUT OF BOUNDS (DEF. 21), OR UNPLAYABLE

1. Lost or out of bounds

a. Procedure

If a ball be lost outside a water hazard or be out of bounds, the player shall play his next stroke as nearly as possible at the spot from which the original ball was played or moved by him, *adding a penalty stroke* to his score for the hole.

If the original stroke was played from the teeing ground, a ball may be teed anywhere within the teeing ground ; if from through the green or a hazard, it shall be dropped ; if on the putting green, it shall be placed.

(Ball in casual water, etc.—Rule 32.)

(Ball in a water hazard—Rule 33-2, 3.)

b. Ascertaining location

A player has the right at any time of ascertaining whether his opponent's ball is out of bounds.

A person outside the match may point out the location of a ball for which search is being made.

c. Standing out of bounds

A player may stand out of bounds to play a ball lying within bounds.

2. Unplayable

a. Player sole judge

The player is the sole judge as to whether his ball is unplayable. It may be declared unplayable at any place on the course.

b. Procedure

If the player deem his ball to be unplayable, he shall either:—

(i) Play his next stroke as provided in Clause 1a of this Rule (stroke-and-distance penalty),

or

(ii) Drop a ball, *under penalty of two strokes*, either (a) within two club-lengths of the point where the ball lay, but not nearer the hole, or (b) behind the point where the ball lay, keeping that point between himself and the hole, with no limit to how far behind that point the ball may be dropped.

Exceptions:—
Ball in casual water, etc.—Rule 32.
Ball in water hazard—Rule 33-2, 3.
(Ball unfit for play—Rule 28.)

3. Provisional ball

A provisional ball for a ball lost, out of bounds or unplayable may be played as provided for in Rule 30.

Penalty for breach of Rule:

Match play—Loss of hole; *Stroke play—Two strokes

*NOTE 1: A serious breach of this Rule should be dealt with by the Committee under Rule 1.

NOTE 2: The penalty stroke provided for in Rule 29-1 may not be remitted by Local Rule.

RULE 30. PROVISIONAL BALL

1. Procedure

If a ball may be lost ouside a water hazard, or may be out of bounds or unplayable, to save time the player may at once play another ball provisionally as nearly as possible from the spot at which the original ball was played. If the original ball was played from the teeing ground, a ball may be teed anywhere within the teeing ground ; if from through the green or a hazard, it shall be dropped ; if on the putting green, it shall be placed.

a. Before playing a provisional ball, the player must announce his intention to his opponent or his marker. The player is not obliged to state the reason for which he plays a provisional ball. He may not restrict the purpose for which it is played.

b. A provisional ball may be played only before the player or his partner goes forward to search for the original ball.

c. Play of a provisional ball from the teeing ground does not affect the order in which the sides play (Rule 12-2).

d. A provisional ball is never an outside agency.

2. Play of provisional ball

The player may play a provisional ball until he reaches the place where the original ball is likely to be.

If the original ball be lost outside a water hazard, or be out of bounds or unplayable, he shall continue play with the provisional ball under penalty provided for in Rule 29-1.

If the original ball be not lost, out of bounds, or unplayable, or if it be in or be lost in a water hazard or a lateral water hazard, the provisional ball shall be abandoned.

3. Ball unplayable : Option prohibited

If a player play a provisional ball under this Rule and deem his first ball unplayable, he must continue playing with the provisional ball ; he may not then proceed under Rule 29-2b.

Penalty for breach of Rule:

Match play—Loss of hole; Stroke play—Two strokes

SECTION VIII

THE RULES OF PLAY

RULE 31. OBSTRUCTIONS (DEF. 20)

1. Movable obstruction may be removed

Any movable obstruction may be removed. If the ball be moved in so doing, it shall be replaced on the exact spot from which it was moved, without penalty. If it be impossible to determine the spot or to replace the ball on the exact spot from which it was moved, the ball shall, through the green or in a hazard, be dropped, or on the putting green be placed, as near as possible to the spot from which it was moved but not nearer the hole, without penalty.

When a ball is in motion, an obstruction other than an attended flagstick and equipment of the players shall not be removed.

2. Interference by immovable obstruction

When the ball lies on or touches an immovable obstruction, or when an immovable obstruction within two club-lengths of the ball interferes with the player's stance, stroke or backward movement of his club for the stroke in the direction in which he wishes to play, the ball may be lifted without penalty. Through the green or in a hazard, the ball shall be dropped, or on the putting green placed, within two club-lengths of that point on the outside of the obstruction nearest which the ball originally lay ; it must not come to rest in, on or touching the obstruction or nearer the hole than its original position.

The player may not measure over, through or under the obstruction.

Interference with the line of play is not of itself interference under this Rule.

(Ball in hazard—Rule 22-2a.)

Penalty for breach of Rule:
Match play—Loss of hole; Stroke play—Two strokes

RULE 32. CASUAL WATER (DEF. 8)
GROUND UNDER REPAIR (DEF. 13)
HOLE MADE BY BURROWING ANIMAL

1. Ball lying in or touching

If a player's ball lie in or touch casual water, ground under repair, or a hole, cast or runway made by a burrowing animal, a reptile or a bird, the player may obtain relief as follows :—

a. Through the green

Through the green, the player may lift and drop the ball without penalty as near as possible to the spot where it lay, but not nearer the hole, on ground which avoids these conditions.

b. In a hazard

In a hazard, the player may lift and drop the ball either :—
Without penalty, in the hazard as near as possible to the spot where the ball lay, but not nearer the hole, on ground which affords maximum relief from these conditions,

or

Under penalty of one stroke, behind the hazard as near as possible to the spot where the ball lay, but not nearer the hole, keeping the hazard between the player and the hole.

c. On the putting green

On the putting green, or if such conditions intervene between a ball lying on the putting green and the hole, the player may lift the ball and place it without penalty in the nearest position to where it lay which affords maximum relief from these conditions, but not nearer the hole.

2. Interference

If any of the conditions covered by this Rule interfere with the player's stance, stroke, or the backward movement of his club for the stroke, the ball may be treated as in Clause 1.

F

3. Ball lost

If a ball be lost under a condition covered by this Rule, except in a hazard, a ball may be dropped without penalty as near as possible to the spot at which the ball last crossed the margin of the area, on ground which avoids these conditions, but not nearer the hole.

If a ball be lost in a hazard, the player may drop a ball either :—

Without penalty, in the hazard, but not nearer the hole than the spot at which the ball last crossed the margin of the area, on ground which affords maximum relief from these conditions;

or

Under penalty of one stroke, outside the hazard, but not nearer the hole, keeping the spot at which the ball last crossed the margin of the hazard between himself and the hole.

In order that a ball may be treated as lost, there must be reasonable evidence to that effect.

4. Re-dropping

If a ball, when dropped, roll into a position covered by this Rule, it may be re-dropped without penalty.   If it be impossible to drop a ball so that it will not roll into such condition, it shall be placed.

Penalty for breach of Rule:
Match play—Loss of hole; Stroke play—Two strokes

SECTION IX

THE RULES OF PLAY

RULE 33. HAZARDS AND WATER HAZARDS (DEF. 14)

1. Touching hazard prohibited

When a ball lies in or touches a hazard or a water hazard, nothing shall be done which may in any way improve its lie.

Before making a stroke, the player shall not touch the ground in the hazard or water with a club or otherwise, nor touch or move a loose impediment lying in or touching the hazard, nor test the condition of the hazard or of any similar hazard ; subject to the following considerations :—

a. Stance

The player may place his feet firmly in taking his stance.

b. Touching fixed or growing object

In addressing the ball or in the stroke or in the backward movement for the stroke, the club may touch any wooden or stone wall, paling or other fixed object or any grass, bush, tree, or other growing substance (but the club may not be soled in the hazard).

c. Obstructions

The player is entitled to relief from obstructions under the provisions of Rule 31.

d. Loose impediment outside hazard

Any loose impediment not in or touching the hazard may be removed.

e. Finding ball

If the ball be covered by sand, fallen leaves or the like, the player may remove as much thereof as will enable him to see the top of the ball ; if the ball be moved in such removal, no penalty shall be incurred, and the ball shall be replaced. The ball may not be lifted for identification.

f. Placing clubs in hazard

The player may, without penalty, place his clubs in the hazard prior to making a stroke, provided nothing is done which may improve the lie of the ball or constitute testing the soil.

g. Smoothing irregularities

After playing a stroke, there is no penalty should the player smooth irregularities in the hazard made by footprints or the soil displaced by a stroke, provided nothing is done that improves the lie of the ball or assists the player in his subsequent play of the hole.

h. Casual water, ground under repair

The player is entitled to relief from casual water, ground under repair, and otherwise as provided for in Rule 32.

i. Interference by a ball

The player is entitled to relief from interference by another ball under the provisions of Rule 24.

2. Ball in water hazard

If a ball lie or be lost in a water hazard (whether the ball lie in water or not), the player may drop a ball, *under penalty of one stroke*, either :—

    a. Behind the water hazard, keeping the spot at which the

ball last crossed the margin of the water hazard between himself and the hole, and with no limit to how far behind the water hazard the ball may be dropped,

or

b. As near as possible to the spot from which the original ball was played; if the stroke was played from the teeing ground, the ball may be teed anywhere within the teeing ground.

NOTE: If a ball has been played from within a water hazard and has not crossed any margin of the hazard, the player may drop a ball behind the hazard under Rule 33-2a.

3. Ball in lateral water hazard (Def. 14-c)

If a ball lie or be lost in a lateral water hazard, the player may, *under penalty of one stroke*, either:—

a. Play his next stroke in accordance with Clause 2a or 2b of this Rule,

or

b. Drop a ball within two club-lengths of the margin of either side of the lateral water hazard, opposite the point where the ball last crossed the hazard margin. The ball must come to rest not nearer the hole than that point.

NOTE: If a ball has been played from within a lateral water hazard and has not crossed any margin of the hazard, the player may drop a ball outside the hazard under Rule 33-3b.

Penalty for breach of Rule:

Match play—Loss of hole; * Stroke play—Two strokes

*NOTE 1: A serious breach of this Rule should be dealt with by the Committee under Rule 1.

NOTE 2: It is a question of fact whether a ball lost after having been struck toward a water hazard is lost inside or outside the hazard. In order to treat the ball as lost in the hazard, there must be reasonable evidence that the ball lodged therein. In the absence of such evidence, the ball must be treated as a lost ball and Rule 29-1 applies.

SECTION X

THE RULES OF PLAY

RULE 34. THE FLAGSTICK (DEF. 12)

1. Flagstick attended, removed or held up

The player may have the flagstick attended, removed or held up to indicate the position of the hole. This may be done only on the authority of the player before he plays his stroke.

If the flagstick be attended or removed by an opponent, a fellow-competitor or the caddie of either with the knowledge of the player and no objection is made, the player shall be deemed to have authorized it.

The player may not require an opponent or a fellow-competitor or his caddie to attend or remove the flagstick.

If a player or a caddie attend or remove the flagstick or stand near the hole while a stroke is being played, he shall be deemed to attend the flagstick until the ball comes to rest.

If the flagstick be not attended before the stroke is played, it shall not be attended or removed while the ball is in motion.

2. Unauthorized attendance

a. Match play

In match play, an opponent or his caddie shall not attend the flagstick without the knowledge or authority of the player.

b. Stroke play

In stroke play, if a fellow-competitor or his caddie attend the flagstick without the knowledge or authority of the competitor, and if the ball strike the flagstick or the person attending it, it is a rub of the green, there is no penalty, and the ball shall be played as it lies.

3. Adjustment of flagstick

Before the player plays his stroke, he or his caddie may adjust the flagstick by placing it in its normal position in the centre of the hole and as nearly upright as possible.

Penalty for breach of Rule 34-1, 2 and 3:
Match play—Loss of hole; Stroke play—Two strokes

4. Ball striking flagstick

a. Flagstick attended

If a player's ball strike the flagstick when it is attended or has been removed or if it strike the person attending the flagstick or equipment carried by him, the player shall incur a penalty of:—

Match play—Loss of hole; Stroke play—Two strokes,
and the ball shall be played as it lies.

b. Flagstick unattended

The player incurs no penalty if his ball strike the flagstick when it is not attended and is in the hole.

5. Ball resting against flagstick

If the ball rest against the flagstick when it is in the hole, the player shall be entitled to have the flagstick removed, and if

F*

the ball fall into the hole the player shall be deemed to have holed out at his last stroke.

NOTE: A referee, observer, marker, steward or other outside agency should not attend the flagstick.

SECTION XI

THE RULES OF PLAY

RULE 35. THE PUTTING GREEN (DEF. 25)

1. General

a. Touching line of putt

The line of the putt must not be touched except as provided in Clauses 1b, 1c and 1d of this Rule, but the player may place the club in front of the ball in addressing it without pressing anything down.

b. Loose impediments

The player may remove any loose impediment on the putting green by picking it up or brushing it aside with his hand or a club without pressing anything down. If the ball be moved, it shall be replaced, without penalty.

c. Repair of ball marks

The player may repair damage to the putting green caused by the impact of a ball. The ball may be lifted to permit repair and shall be replaced on the spot from which it was lifted ; in match play the ball must be replaced immediately if the opponent so requests.

If a ball be moved during such repair, it shall be replaced, without penalty.

d. Cleaning ball

A ball lying on the putting green may be lifted and cleaned, without penalty, and replaced on the spot from which it was lifted ; in match play the ball must be replaced immediately if the opponent so requests.

e. Direction for putting

When the player's ball is on the putting green, the player's caddie, his partner or his partner's caddie may, before the stroke is played, point out a line for putting, but the line of the putt shall not be touched in front of, to the side of, or behind the hole.

No mark shall be placed anywhere on the putting green to indicate a line for putting.

f. Testing surface

During the play of a hole, a player shall not test the surface of the putting green by rolling a ball or roughening or scraping the surface.

g. Other ball to be at rest

The player shall not play until his opponent's or fellow-competitor's ball is at rest.

h. Ball overhanging hole

When any part of the ball overhangs the edge of the hole, the owner of the ball is not allowed more than a few seconds to determine whether it is at rest. If by then the ball has not fallen into the hole, it is deemed to be at rest.

i. Lifting other ball prohibited

While the player's ball is in motion, an opponent's or fellow-competitor's ball shall not be lifted or touched.

j. Ball on a wrong putting green

A ball lying on a putting green other than that of the hole being played must be lifted and dropped off the putting green as near as possible to where the ball lay but not nearer the hole and not in a hazard, without penalty.

k. Ball played as it lies and not touched

For ball purposely moved or purposely touched, see Rule 16.

Penalty for breach of Rule 35-1:

Match play—Loss of hole; Stroke play—Two strokes

NOTE: When a ball on the putting green is to be lifted, its position should be marked. A recommended method of marking is to place a small coin or similar object immediately behind the ball; if it interfere with another player, it should be moved one or more putterhead-lengths to one side.

2. Match play

a. Ball interfering with play

When the ball nearer the hole lies on the putting green, if the player consider that the opponent's ball might interfere with his play, the player may require the opponent to lift his ball, without penalty.

The opponent shall replace his ball after the player has played his stroke. If the player's ball stop on the spot formerly occupied by the lifted ball, the player shall first play another stroke before the lifted ball is replaced.

If the player's ball be accidentally touched or moved in complying with this Rule, no penalty shall be incurred and the ball if moved shall be replaced.

b. **Playing out of turn**

If a player play when his opponent should have done so, the opponent may immediately require the player to replay the stroke, in which case the player shall replace his ball and play in correct order, without penalty.

c. **Opponent's ball displaced**

If the player's ball knock the opponent's ball into the hole, the opponent shall be deemed to have holed out at his last stroke.

If the player's ball move the opponent's ball, the opponent may replace it, but this must be done before another stroke is played by either side. If the player's ball stop on the spot formerly occupied by the opponent's ball, and the opponent declare his intention to replace his ball, the player shall first play another stroke, after which the opponent shall replace his ball.

(Three-Ball, Best-Ball and Four-Ball match play—Rule 40-1c.)

d. **Conceding opponent's next stroke**

When the opponent's ball has come to rest (Rule 35-1h), the player may concede the opponent to have holed out with his next stroke and may remove the opponent's ball with a club or otherwise. If the player does not concede the opponent's next stroke and the opponent's ball fall into the hole, the opponent shall be deemed to have holed out with his last stroke.

If the opponent's next stroke has not been conceded, the opponent shall play without delay in correct order.

Penalty for breach of Rule 35-2—Loss of hole

3. **Stroke play**

a. **Ball interfering with play**

When the ball nearer the hole lies on the putting green, if the competitor consider that the fellow-competitor's ball might interfere with his play, the competitor may require the fellow-competitor to lift or play his ball, at the option of its owner, without penalty.

If the owner of the ball refuse to comply with the Rule when required to do so, the competitor making the request may lift the ball, and *the owner of the ball shall be disqualified.*

NOTE: It is recommended that the ball nearer the hole be played, rather than lifted, unless the subsequent play of a fellow-competitor is likely to be affected.

b. Ball assisting play

If the fellow-competitor consider that his ball lying on the putting green might be of assistance to the competitor, the fellow-competitor may lift or play first, without penalty.

c. Ball striking fellow-competitor's ball

When both balls lie on the putting green or within twenty yards of the hole, if the competitor's ball strike a fellow-competitor's ball not lying in a hazard, *the competitor shall incur a penalty of two strokes* and shall play his ball as it lies. The fellow-competitor's ball shall be at once replaced.

d. Ball lifted before holed out

For ball lifted before holed out, see Rule 22-1b.

SECTION XII

THE RULES OF PLAY

RULE 36. THE COMMITTEE (DEF. 9)

1. Conditions

The Committee shall lay down the conditions under which a competition is to be played.

Certain special rules governing stroke play are so substantially different from those governing match play that combining the two forms of play is not practicable and is not permitted. The results of matches played and the scores returned in these circumstances shall not be accepted.

2. Order and times of starting

a. General

The Committee shall arrange the order and times of starting, which, when possible, shall be decided by lot.

b. Match play

When a competition is played over an extended period, the Committee shall lay down the limit of time within which each round shall be completed.

When players are allowed to arrange the date of their match within these limits, the Committee should announce that the match must be played at a stated hour on the last day of the period unless the players agree to a prior date.

c. Stroke play

Competitors shall play in couples unless the Committee authorizes play by threes or fours. If there be a single competitor, the Committee shall provide him with a player who shall mark for him, or provide a marker and allow him to compete alone, or allow him to compete with another group.

3. Decision of ties

The Committee shall announce the manner, day and time for the decision of a halved match or of a tie, whether played on level terms or under handicap.

A halved match shall not be decided by stroke play. A tie in stroke play shall not be decided by a match.

4. The course

a. New holes

New holes should be made on the day on which a stroke competition begins, and at such other times as the Committee considers necessary provided all competitors in a single round play with each hole cut in the same position.

b. Practice ground

Where there is no practice ground available outside the area of a competition course, the Committee shall lay down the area on which players may practice on any day of a competition if it is practicable to do so.

On any day of a stroke competition, the Committee should not normally permit practice on or to a putting green or from a hazard of the competition course.

c. Course unplayable

If the Committee or its authorized representative consider that the course is not in a playable condition, or that insufficient light renders the proper playing of the game impossible, it shall have the power in match and stroke play to order a temporary suspension of play, or in stroke play to declare play null and void and to cancel all scores for the round in question.

When a round is cancelled, all penalties incurred in that round are cancelled.

When play has been temporarily suspended, it shall be resumed from where it was discontinued, even though resumption occur on a subsequent day.

(Procedure in discontinuing play—Rule 37-6b.)

5. Modification of penalty

The Committee has no power to waive a Rule of Golf. A

penalty of disqualification, however, may in exceptional individual cases be waived or be modified or be imposed under Rule 1 if the Committee consider such action warranted.

6. Defining bounds and margins

The Committee shall define accurately :—
    a. The course and out of bounds.
    b. The margins of hazards, water hazards, and lateral water hazards, where there is any doubt.
    c. Ground under repair.
    d. Obstructions.

7. Local Rules
a. Policy

The Committee shall make and publish Local Rules for abnormal conditions, having regard to the policy of the Governing Authority of the country concerned as set forth in the Appendix attached to these Rules.

b. Waiving penalty prohibited

A penalty imposed by a Rule of Golf shall not be waived by a Local Rule.

RULE 37. THE PLAYER

1. Conditions

The player shall be responsible for acquainting himself with the conditions under which the competition is to be played.

2. Caddie and forecaddie

For any breach of a Rule or Local Rule by his caddie, the player incurs the relative penalty.

The player may have only one caddie, *under penalty of disqualification.*

The player may send his own caddie forward to mark the position of any ball.

If a forecaddie be employed by the Committee, he is an outside agency. (Definition 22.)

3. Infringement assisting partner

If a player infringe a Rule or Local Rule so as to assist his partner's play, *the partner incurs the relative penalty in addition to any penalty incurred by the player.*

4. Handicap

Before starting in a handicap competition, the player shall check his handicap from the official list, and in the case of match play or bogey competitions shall inform himself of the holes at which strokes are given or taken.

5. Time and order of starting

Players shall start at the times and in the order arranged by the Committee.

Penalty for breach of Rule 37-5: Disqualification

6. Discontinuance of play

a. When permitted

Players shall not discontinue play on account of bad weather or for any other reason, unless:

They consider that there be danger from lightning,

or

There be some other reason, such as sudden illness, which the Committee considers satisfactory.

If a player discontinues play without specific permission from the Committee, he shall report to the Committee as soon as possible.

General Exception:—Players discontinuing match play by agreement are not subject to disqualification unless by so doing the competition is delayed.

Penalty for breach of Rule 37-6a: Disqualification

b. Procedure

When play is discontinued in accordance with the Rules, it should, if feasible, be discontinued after the completion of the play of a hole. If this is not feasible, the player shall lift his ball after marking the spot on which it lay ; in such case he shall replace the ball on that spot when play is resumed.

Penalty for breach of Rule 37-6b:

*Match play—Loss of hole; *Stroke play—Two strokes*

NOTE: A serious breach of this Rule should be dealt with by the Committee under Rule 1.

7. Undue delay

Players shall at all times play without undue delay.   Between the completion of a hole and driving off the next tee, a player may not delay play in any way.

Penalty for breach of Rule 37-7:

* *Match play—Loss of hole; Stroke play—Two strokes*
For repeated offence—Disqualification

* *NOTE: If the player delay play between holes, he is delaying the play of the next hole, and the penalty applies to that hole.*

8. Refusal to comply with Rule

If a competitor in stroke play refuse to comply with a Rule affecting the rights of another competitor, *he shall be disqualified.*

9. Artificial devices

The player shall not use any artificial device for the purpose of gauging or measuring distance or conditions which might affect his play, *under penalty of disqualification.*

RULE 38. SCORING IN STROKE PLAY

1. Recording scores

The Committee shall issue to each competitor's marker a score card containing the date and the competitor's name.

After each hole the marker shall check the score with the competitor. On completion of the round the marker shall sign the card and hand it to the competitor ; should more than one marker record the scores, each shall sign the part for which he is responsible.

2. Checking scores

The competitor shall check his score for each hole, settle any doubtful points with the Committee, ensure that the marker has signed the card, countersign the card himself, and return it to the Committee as soon as possible.

Penalty for breach of Rule 38-2: Disqualification

The competitor is solely responsible for the correctness of the score recorded for each hole. The Committee is responsible for the addition of scores and application of the correct handicap.

3. No alteration of scores

No alteration may be made on a card after the competitor has returned it to the Committee.

If the competitor return a score for any hole lower than actually played, *he shall be disqualified.*

A score higher than actually played must stand as returned.

RULE 39. BOGEY OR PAR COMPETITIONS

1. Conditions

a. A bogey or a par competition is a form of stroke competition in which play is against a fixed score at each hole of the stipulated round or rounds.

b. The reckoning is made as in match play.

c. The winner is the competitor who is most successful in the aggregate of holes.

G

2. Rules for stroke play apply

The Rules for stroke play shall apply with the following exceptions :—

a. No return at any hole

Any hole for which a competitor makes no return shall be regarded as a loss.

b. Scoring cards

The holes at which strokes are to be given or taken shall be indicated on the card issued by the Committee.

c. Recording scores

The marker shall be responsible for marking only the gross number of strokes at each hole where a competitor makes a net score equal to or less than the fixed score.

3. Disqualification penalties

a. From the competition

A competitor shall be disqualified from the competition for a breach of any of the following :

Rule 2—The Club and the Ball.
Rule 4—Agreement to Waive Rules Prohibited.
Rule 8-3—Practice before Round.
Rule 24—Ball interfering with Play—Stroke Play.
Rule 35-3a—Putting green—Stroke Play, Bill interfering
        with Play.
Rule 37-2—Caddie and Forecaddie.
Rule 37-5—Time and Order of Starting.
Rule 37-6a—Discontinuance of Play.
Rule 37-7—Undue Delay (repeated offence).
Rule 37-8—Refusal to comply with Rule.
Rule 37-9—Artificial devices.
Rule 38-2—Checking Scores.
Rule 38-3—No Alteration of Scores, except that the com-
        petitor shall not be disqualified when a
        breach of this Rule does not affect the result
        of the hole.

b. For a hole

In all other cases where a breach of a Rule would entail disqualification, *the competitor shall be disqualified only for the hole at which the breach occurred.*

(Modifications of Penalty—Rule 36-5.)

SECTION XIII

THE RULES OF PLAY

RULE 40. THREE-BALL, BEST-BALL AND FOUR-BALL MATCH PLAY

1. General

a. Rules of golf apply

The Rules of Golf, so far as they are not at variance with the following special Rules, shall apply to all three-ball, best-ball and four-ball matches.

b. Ball influencing play

Any player may have any ball (except the ball about to be played) lifted or played, at the option of the owner, if he consider that it might interfere with or be of assistance to a player or side, but this is only permissible before the next stroke is played by the player whose turn it is.

c. Ball moved by another ball

If a player's ball move any other ball in the match, the owner of the moved ball shall place the ball on the spot from which it was moved, without penalty, as provided in Rule 27-1a.

d. Playing out of turn

Through the green or in a hazard, a player shall incur no penalty if he play when an opponent should have done so. The stroke shall not be replayed.

On the putting green, if a player play when an opponent should have done so, the opponent may immediately require the player to replay the stroke in correct order, without penalty.

2. Three-ball match play

In a three-ball match, each player is playing two distinct matches.

a. Ball stopped or deflected by an opponent

If a player's ball be stopped or deflected by an opponent, his caddie or equipment, *that opponent shall lose the hole in his match with the player*. The other opponent shall treat the occurrence as a rub of the green (Definition 27).

Exception: Ball striking person attending flagstick—Rule 34-4a.

b. **Ball at rest moved by an opponent**

If the player's ball be touched or moved by an opponent, his caddie or equipment (except as otherwise provided in the Rules), Rule 27-2a applies. *That opponent shall incur a penalty stroke in his match with the player*, but not in his match with the other opponent.

3. **Best-ball and four-ball match play**

a. **Order of play**

Balls belonging to the same side may be played in the order the side considers best.

b. **Ball stopped by player's side**

If a player's ball be stopped or deflected by the player, his partner or either of their caddies or equipment, *the player is disqualified for the hole*. His partner incurs no penalty.

c. **Ball stopped by opponent's side**

If a player's ball be stopped or deflected by an opponent, his caddie or equipment, *the opponent's side shall lose the hole*.

Exception: Ball striking person attending flagstick—Rule 34-4a.

d. **Partner's ball moved by player accidentally**

If a player, his partner, or either of their caddies accidentally move a ball owned by their side or by touching anything cause it to move (except as otherwise provided for in the Rules), *the owner of the ball shall incur a penalty stroke*, but the penalty shall not apply to his partner. The ball shall be played as it lies.

e. **Ball moved by opponent's side**

If a player's ball be touched or moved by an opponent, his caddie or equipment (except as otherwise provided in the Rules), *that opponent shall incur a penalty stroke*, but the penalty shall not apply to the other opponent. The player shall place the ball on the spot from which it was moved, without penalty, as provided in Rule 27-1a.

f. **Maximum of fourteen clubs**

The side shall be penalized for a violation of Rule 3 by either partner.

g. **Disqualification penalties**

A player shall be disqualified from the match for a breach of Rule 37-5 (Time and Order of Starting), but, in the discretion of the Committee, the penalty shall not necessarily apply to his partner (Definition 28—Note).

A side shall be disqualified for a breach of any of the following:

Rule 2—The Club and the Ball.
Rule 4—Agreement to Waive Rules Prohibited.
Rule 37-2—Caddie and Forecaddie.
Rule 37-7—Undue delay (repeated offence).
Rule 37-9—Artificial Devices.

A player shall be disqualified for the hole in question and from the remainder of the match for a breach of Rule 37-6a (Discontinuance of Play), but the penalty shall not apply to his partner.
(Modification of penalty—Rule 36-5.)

h. Infringement assisting partner

If a player infringe a Rule or Local Rule so as to assist his partner's play, *the partner incurs the relative penalty in addition to any penalty incurred by the player.*

i. Penalty applies to player only

In all other cases where, by the Rules of Golf, a player would incur a penalty, the penalty shall not apply to his partner.

RULE 41. FOUR-BALL STROKE PLAY

1. Conditions

a. The Rules of Golf, so far as they are not at variance with the following special Rules, shall apply to four-ball stroke play.

b. In four-ball stroke play two players play as partners, each playing his own ball.

c. The lower score of the partners is the score of the hole. If one partner fail to complete the play of a hole, there is no penalty.

2. Ball influencing play

a. **Lifting permitted.** Any competitor may have any ball (except the ball about to be played) lifted or played, at the option of the owner, if he consider that it might interfere with or be of assistance to a competitor or side, but this is only permissible before the next stroke is played by the competitor whose turn it is.

If the owner of the ball refuse to comply with this Rule when required to do so, *his side shall be disqualified.*

b. **Lifting prohibited.** On the putting green, while the competitor's ball is in motion, any other ball shall not be touched by anyone.

3. Balls to be at rest

On the putting green, the competitor shall not play until all other balls are at rest.

4. Balls struck by another ball

When the balls concerned lie on the putting green or within twenty yards of the hole, if a competitor's ball strike any other ball not lying in a hazard, *the competitor shall incur a penalty of two strokes* and shall play his ball as it lies. The other ball shall be at once replaced.

In all other cases, if a competitor's ball strike any other ball, the competitor shall play his ball as it lies. The owner of the moved ball shall place his ball on the spot from which it was moved, without penalty, as provided in Rule 27-1a.

5. Order of play

Balls belonging to the same side may be played in the order the side considers best.

6. Disqualification penalties

a. From the competition

A competitor shall be disqualified from the competition for a breach of any of the following, but the penalty shall not apply to his partner:

> Rule 8-3—Practice before Round.
> Rule 37-5—Time and Order of Starting.
> Rule 38-3—No Alteration of Scores, except that the competitor shall not be disqualified when a breach of this Rule does not affect the result of the hole.

A side shall be disqualified from the competition for a breach of any of the following:

> Rule 2—The Club and the Ball.
> Rule 4—Agreement to Waive Rules Prohibited.
> Rule 37-2—Caddie and Forecaddie.
> Rule 37-7—Undue Delay (repeated offence).
> Rule 37-8—Refusal to comply with Rule.
> Rule 37-9—Artificial Devices.
> Rule 38-2—Checking Scores.
> Rule 41-2a—Ball Influencing Play, Refusal to Lift.

By both partners, at the same hole, of a Rule or Rules the penalty for which is disqualification either from the competition or for a hole.

b. From the remainder of the competition

A competitor shall be disqualified for the hole in question and from the remainder of the competition for a breach of Rule 37-6a (Discontinuance of Play), but the penalty shall not apply to his partner.

c. For a hole only

In all other cases where a breach of a Rule would entail

disqualification, *the competitor shall be disqualified only for the hole at which the breach occurred.*

(Modification of Penalty—Rule 36-5.)

7. Infringement assisting partner

If a competitor infringe a Rule or Local Rule so as to assist his partner's play, *the partner incurs the relative penalty in addition to any penalty incurred by the competitor.*

8. Penalty applies to competitor only

In all other cases where, by the Rules of Golf, a competitor would incur a penalty, the penalty shall not apply to his partner.

APPENDIX I.

LOCAL RULES

Committees in charge of courses shall, when considered necessary,

1. Make Local Rules for such abnormal conditions as:
    a. Existence of mud.
    b. Accumulation of leaves.
    c. Damage caused to the course by animals.
    d. Local conditions which could be held to interfere with the proper playing of the Game. If this necessitates modification of a Rule of Golf the approval of the Governing Authority must be obtained.
    e. Conditions which make a Local Rule necessary for the preservation of the course ; this includes prohibition, where necessary, of playing a ball lying in ground under repair.
    f. Obstructions, their limits and the extent of relief of the application of Rule 31 is impracticable.
    g. Any construction which the Committee considers an integral part of the course (Def. 20d), and defines as not an obstruction.
2. Frame regulations governing Priority on the Course.
3. Frame regulations governing the practice area during Stroke Competitions. (Rules 8-3, 36-4b.)

For the Royal and Ancient Golf Club
of St. Andrews.

BRIGADIER E. BLICKMAN, D.S.O.
Secretary.

INDEX TO THE RULES

Note : For the sake of clarity in this index, clauses of Rules are shown in brackets so—(6) ; and sub-clauses not in brackets so—a.